MAGDALENE QUESTION

OTHER WRITINGS OF DR. KETTER

Die Versuchung Jesu nach dem Berichte der Synoptiker, XX, und 140 Seiten, gr. 8° (Neutestamentl. Abhandlungen, Bd. 6, Heft 3). Münster i. W., Aschendorffsche Verlagsbuchhandlung, 1918.

Das Herz des Gottmenschen im Weltenplane. Eine Begründung der Herz-Jesu-Verehrung für Freund und Feind. Von Dr. P. J. Pörtzgen. Vierte Auflage neubearbeitet von Prof. Dr. P. Ketter. 208 Seiten, gr. 8°. Verlag der Paulinus-Druckerei, Trier, 1926.

Im Lande der Offenbarung. Reiseschilderungen aus dem Orient. Mit 50 Bildern nach Originalaufnahmen und zwei Karten. Zweite, vermehrte Auflage (4–5 Tausend). 268 Seiten, gr. 8°. Verlag der Paulinus-Druckerei, Trier, 1931.

Christus und die Frauen. Frauenleben und Frauengestalten im Neuen Testament, XV, und 412 Seiten, gr. 8°. Verbandsverlag weiblicher Vereine, Düsseldorf, 1933.

The
Magdalene Question

Translated from the German
"DIE MAGDALENEN FRAGE"

of

DR. PETER KETTER
Professor of Theology at Trier

By
REV. HUGO C. KOEHLER, M.A.

Catholic Authors Press
Hartford

Nihil obstat:
ALOYSIUS J. MUENCH, LL.D.
Censor Deputatus

Imprimatur:
✠ SAMUEL A. STRITCH,
Archiepiscopus Milwaukiensis

July 10, 1935

FOREWORD

The theme of Mary Magdalene is known to every Christian.

The accepted theory is that she was a woman of sin, from whom Christ cast out seven devils, thereby restoring her to the life of grace.

In the popular theory she became a most faithful follower of Christ, was present at the Crucifixion, and was the first recorded person to see the risen Lord. This theory cannot claim a great antiquity, but in the Middle Ages, and after, it is the most common opinion.

The opinion was helped by sentiment. The converted Magdalene with her subsequent great love of Christ offered herself as a luminous example of the power of penance.

The accord with which the traditional opinion was received by preachers and ascetics was not endorsed by the deeper theologians. The profounder exegesis reveals that the Magdalene of the preachers and the prayer books agrees not with the Magdalene of the Holy Scriptures. Through a false idea of piety some theologians kept silent: others spoke with clear arguments against tradition.

In his Brochure, *Die Magdalenen Frage* (The Magdalene Question) Dr. Peter Ketter, professor of theology in Trier, submits the whole question to a searching analysis. His treatment is eminently fair and unbiased.

He has the right temper of mind for an apologist: "he plays the ball, not the man." There has not appeared at any time a profounder and more logical treatise.

An English translation shall bring this excellent treatise to a larger public. This is the motive of the present publication. Though there be many books, there is always place for a better book.

If Dr. Ketter's thesis shall stand, it shall remove from Catholic fields of thought an ugly error.

ANDREW E. BREEN

PREFACE

Various discussions with Bishop M. Felix Korum gave the impetus for this treatise. Until his death, he was wont to discuss scientific questions with his private secretary. The manuscript was already prepared for the press when Urban Holzmeister, S.J., published his findings on the Magdalene Question in Christian Tradition.[1] His work was completed by an examination of the Biblical narratives by Joseph Sickenberger,[2] and W. Müller.[3] All three confirm the results which I had already written down during the war. It is to be hoped, therefore, that the wish I implied in a work on my tour in the Orient may be fulfilled: "On the site of the poor village El-Medjdel once stood the flourishing Magdala; the home of one of Jesus' most devoted followers, Mary Magdalene. It will, no doubt, take a long time before we shall cease identifying this renowned lady of Magdala with the sinful woman in the Gospel, whose name and residence are unknown to us."[4] No remark in the entire book caused so many oral and written inquiries as these two sentences. This led me to further researches, since it was a sign that there existed a widespread interest in

---

[1]*Zeitschr. f. Kath. Theol.*, 46 (1922), pp. 402–22; 556–84.
[2]*Bibl. Zeitschr.*, 17 (1925–26), pp. 63–74.
[3]*Der Fels*, 21 (1926–27), pp. 85–94; 131–38.
[4]*Im Lande der Offenbarung* (Trier, 1927), p. 63.

this question. The section on the tradition of the Fathers could be shortened with a reference to the work of Holzmeister.

The findings first appeared in three installments in the magazine *Pastor Bonus,* 40 (1929). In answer to many requests, the articles were printed in a brochure.

THE AUTHOR

Trier, Feast of Mary Magdalene, 1929.
Imprimatur: Treviris, die 15 Julii, 1929.
Vicarius in spir. Generalis Tilmann.

TRANSLATOR'S NOTE

The translator wishes to express his thanks to the author, Dr. Peter Ketter, for his willing consent to have the brochure translated into English. Thanks are likewise due to the Rev. Dr. Andrew E. Breen, the Rt. Rev. Msgr. Aloysius J. Muench, and the Rev. Raymond W. Hietpas.

SUGGESTED READINGS

Breen, Andrew E., *A Harmonized Exposition of the Four Gospels,* 3rd rev. ed. (1928): Vol. II, pp. 344–353; Vol. III, pp. 193–196; 415; Vol. IV, pp. 554 ff.

Gorman, Ralph C. P., "Mary Magdalen," in *The Sign,* Vol. 14, No. 7, p. 425 f.

Thurston, Herbert, S.J., "St. Mary Magdalene and the Early Saints of Provence," in *The Month,* Jan., 1899, pp. 75–81.

Thurston, Herbert, S.J., "Relics, Authentic and Spurious," in *The Month,* June, 1930, pp. 543, 544.

Thurston, Herbert, S.J., "St. Mary Magdalene—Fact and Legend," in *Studies,* Vol. XXIII (1934), p. 110 ff.

CONTENTS

PAGE

FOREWORD 5

PREFACE 7

TRANSLATOR'S NOTE 9

SUGGESTED READINGS 10

INTRODUCTION 15

A HARMONY OF THE GOSPEL MATERIAL 22

Is Mary Magdalene Identical with the Sinful
Woman? 27

Is the Sinful Woman Identical with Mary of
Bethany? 38

Is Mary Magdalene the Same as Mary of
Bethany? 56

TRADITION 66

The Opinions of the Fathers of the Church and
Early Theologians 66

Ecclesiastical Office and Representation of Art . 80

THE MAGDALENE QUESTION IN PRESENT-
DAY BIBLICAL CRITICISM 92

MAGDALENE QUESTION

INTRODUCTION

"After her death, Mary Magdalene, the faithful follower of the Lord, met with a double misfortune: she
was robbed of her good reputation, being accused of
sins which she never committed, and furthermore, she
was deprived of her individual personality, since she and
two other women in the Gospel narrative are taken for
one person on account of their names. The first took
place through her identification with the 'great sinner'
mentioned in Luke 7; the other through her confusion
with Mary of Bethany."

Thus Karl Burger begins one of his articles on Mary
Magdalene, and thereby touches upon a question with
which spiritual writers have been occupied since Patristic
times.[1]

Easy though it may seem from the words of Burger,
the answer cannot be given by yes or no. The defenders
of the difference of persons must prove their thesis to
those who, even today, relying on notable witnesses of
tradition, still hold Mary Magdalene, Mary of Bethany,
and the sinful woman to be one and the same person.
From childhood, she has been held up to us in sermons
and instructions as the example of true conversion and

---

[1] In *Realenzyklopädie f. pr. Theol. u. Kirche* XII[3] (Leipzig, 1903),
336. Cf. A. W. Kerr, *The two Marys of Bethany and Magdala,
wronged for 15 centuries* (London, 1922).

of enduring penitence, in the same class with Peter and David. There is scarcely any more striking picture of divine Mercy and the love of the Saviour for sinners than this woman, who, if she be taken as the same person as the sinful woman known in the city, appears before Christ, anoints His feet, receives forgiveness of her many sins because she loved much, then out of gratitude becomes a zealous follower of the Lord; whose sister is Martha, the mistress of the house, busied about many things, while Mary sits at the feet of the Master and receives His praise because she chose the better part; who, six days before the passion, again anoints our Lord; who remains faithful even beneath the cross; who on Easter morn hurries to the sepulcher, tearfully seeks the Master, and is found worthy by Him to have a special apparition; who, according to the Provençal tradition, is placed with her sister Martha and her brother Lazarus on a pilotless ship which miraculously lands in Southern France where she spends the last days of her life doing penance in the grotto of Sainte-Baume. In works of art, in stories, and in religious books, we find the same person portrayed in all these distinct scenes. Most frequently she bears the name Mary Magdalene or simply the Magdalene. She is also depicted as Mary of Bethany, as Mary, the sister of Martha and Lazarus, or as the "sinful woman."

Every theologian must take some stand on this question.[2] The ecclesiastical magisterium gives each one perfect liberty to uphold the opinion of those who say that one person bore various names, or to join those who

---

[2] In the *Monatsboten für die Katholische Geistlichkeit*, 21 (1929), 58–60, there is a very uncritical presentation.

make a distinction of several persons. A conclusive solution has as yet not been found or universally accepted, and P. Nisius believes that this controverted point will never be solved.[3] The following observations will combine the known elements with those less known or with unnoticed historical facts, and thus contribute to a clearer understanding of the question.

The material to be employed comes to us from two sources, from the Gospels and from tradition. A definite solution could be effected either from a uniform explanation of the respective passages of the Bible, or from a unanimous and constant tradition. The tradition of the Fathers on this question, however, is for the most part only an explanation of the Gospel narratives, leaning now to one side, then to the other. In the Latin Church, for a long time after the time of Gregory the Great, the opinion for one person with various names found the greatest support. In the latter part of the Middle Ages and also in modern times this conception was strongly favored especially in France, after the tradition concerning the arrival and activities of the three persons of Bethany in France had become firmly established.[4] But there also arose the dissenting voices of French scholars who were in favor of the non-identification of the three women. Jacques Lefèvre was the first to attempt to prove the difference of persons, as he did in his work, *De tri-*

---

[3]Cf. M. Buchberger, *Kirchl. Handlexikon,* II (Freiburg, 1912), p. 822. Similarly A. Durand remarks: "Le problème est insoluble." *Evangile selon S. Jean* (Paris, 1927), p. 333.

[4]Cf. especially M. Faillon, *Monuments inédits sur l'apostolat de Ste. Marie Madeleine en Provence,* 2 vol. (Paris, 1865); *Acta Sanctorum,* Julii V, pp. 187–225; Duchesne, *Fastes Ep. I²*, pp. 321–40.

bus et unica Magdalena.[5] The book caused so much
excitement that the Sorbonne, on November 9, 1521,
placed it under censure, and forbade the teaching of
Lefèvre's opinion, since exclusively the identity of the
three women "amplectendam esse et tenendam, ut Evangelio Christi conformem et Ecclesiae Catholicae ritui
consentaneam."[6] Lefèvre certainly went too far, especially in his polemic against the authority of Gregory
the Great and in the form of his arguments; but the
weak counter arguments in the writings of the Sorbonne
convinced scarcely anyone. Thus it happened that soon
afterwards eminent members of the Sorbonne itself stood
for the distinction of persons.

A vast amount of literature was written especially in
France on the question of the Magdalene.

The *Analecta Bollandiana* continually contain new
declarations and discussions.

Duchesne, through his criticism of the Provençal tradition, aroused to action many defenders of the traditional
opinion, who wished to save the tottering foundation of
an opinion whose scientific equipment is in part very im-
perfect. H. Delehaye, S.J., in the following words com-
ments on the work of A. Pissier, *Le culte de S. Marie-
Madeleine à Vezelay* (1923): "Il serait temps d'en finir
avec de pareils arguments et de ne plus rappeler, entre

---

[5]Paris, 1517–19.

[6]This is found in *Acta Sanctorum, l.c.,* pp. 189–90. Two years after
the publication of Lefèvre's book, Bishop John Fisher of Rochester
wrote an article *"De unica Maria"* against Lefèvre. The Spaniard
Balthasar Socco followed him in a work *De triplice Maria,* which
appeared in Germany.

gens sérieux, cette agréable boutade, autrement que pour en sourire."[7]

Touching an investigation of E. Vacandard,[8] this same learned Bollandist remarks, after an acknowledgment of the careful demonstration of the author: "Il faut être singulièrement étranger aux études historiques pour maintenir, après cela, la vieille thèse si souvent réfutée. Certains esprits timides ferment inconsciemment les yeux à la lumière, parce qu'ils redoutent les conséquences d'une adhésion et s'imaginent d'ébranler la dévotion elle-même."[9]

Thirty years earlier it was declared in the *Analecta* that: "Il n'est plus d'écrivain tant soit peu sérieux qui accorde encore quelque valeur historique aux récits relatifs au séjour de Lazare et de ses soeurs en Provence. Les Provençaux, cela s'entend, font d'ordinaire exception, et avec eux quelques incorrigibles aveugles qui ne veulent point voir."[10]

In the French literature defending the Provençal tradi-

---

[7]"It is time to lay aside such arguments, and no more to repeat among intelligent persons this whim, save to elicit a smile thereon."

[8]"La venue de Lazare et de Marie-Madeleine en Provence," in *Revue des questions historiques,* 100 (1924), pp. 257–303.

[9]"One must be much a stranger to historical studies to maintain, after such demonstration, the old theory so often refuted. Some timid souls unconsciously close their eyes to the light, because they fear the consequences of accepting [the demonstration], and they imagine that thus they should destroy the cult." *Analecta Boll.,* 42 (1924), p. 460.

[10]"There is no historian so superficial who will attribute any historical value to the story of the sojourn of Lazarus and of his sisters in Provence. Of course, the inhabitants of Provence, for the most part, form an exception, and with them some invincible blind persons, who are unwilling to see." *Ana.* 12 (1893), p. 296.

tion, nationalistic sentiments are sometimes so strong that it would seem that France's renown and reputation stand or fall with this tradition.

The truth of this tradition is only indirectly disturbed by the question whether Mary Magdalene be the same as Mary the sister of Martha, or whether she be the same as the anonymous sinner.[11] If the Provençal tradition were real history, and not legendary, we should have in it the strongest evidence of the identity of the three women, since in it Mary Magdalene appears as the sister of Lazarus and as the converted sinner.

---

[11]Shall anyone therefore approve the view of Francis Plaine who made the bold assertion: *"Ceux qui révoquent en doute l'authenticité de la venue et du séjour de Madeleine en Provence, accusent équivalem-ment l'Eglise de n' avoir pas répondu aux intentions de son divin Fondateur; le Maitre n'a-t-il pas dit en effet: Ubicumque praedicatum fuerit hoc evangelium in universo mundo, et quod haec fecit narrabitur [Mk. 14:9]? Cf. Analecta Bolland. 16 [1897], 516.* (They who doubt the authenticity of the coming and sojourn of the Magdalene in Prov-ence in effect accuse the Church of failure to fulfill the will of her divine Founder. Has not the Master said: Wheresoever this Gospel shall be preached in the whole world, also this which she has done shall be spoken of. Mk. 14:9)? To this remark, the Bollandists answer: *"Ceci serait tout simplement ridicule, s'il n'était plus regrettable encore de voir faire un abus aussi criant des paroles sacrées."* [*Id.*]. (This should be merely ridiculous, were it not for the more regrettable abuse of the sacred words.) He could have shown that "the whole world" without further ado does not agree with France and Provence, as it would seem from Plaine. The contrary legends of Aix, Vezelay, Mar-seille, and Tarascon show that due to their pious beliefs coupled with local patriotism the people tried to prove that the establishment of cloisters and bishoprics dated back to apostolic times. Gregory of Tours should have known something of the Magdalene's tomb in southern France, yet he speaks of her resting place in Ephesus (Cf. H. Bruders, S.J., "Die geschichtliche Kirchenverfassung in Gallien und am Rhein in Gegensatz zu den apostolischen Legenden," in: *Bonner Zeitschrift f. Theol. u. Seelsorge 4*, [*1927*], *197–218*).

There are six possible hypotheses, and each one has found its defenders (Urban Holzmeister gives a list of authors for the first five hypotheses, see *Zeitschr. f. kath. Theol.* 46 [1922] 403–406):

1. The three women are identical.

2. They are three distinct persons.

3. Mary Magdalene is the same as the sinful woman, but different from Mary of Bethany.

4. Mary Magdalene is identical with Mary of Bethany, distinct from the sinful woman.

5. Mary of Bethany and the sinful woman are one, but different from Mary Magdalene.

6. Judgment remains suspended; no hypothesis can be demonstrated to be the correct one.

If we wish to form a judgment on this question, two sources are at our disposal: (1) an examination of the Gospel narratives; (2) an estimation of ecclesiastical tradition as expressed in the Fathers as well as in liturgy and in art.

A HARMONY OF THE GOSPEL MATERIAL

THE SINFUL WOMAN
Luke 7:36-50

36. And one of the Pharisees desired Him to eat with him. And He went into the house of the Pharisee, and sat down to meat.

37. And behold a woman that was in the city, a sinner, when she knew that He sat at meat in the Pharisee's house, brought an alabaster box of ointment;

38. And standing behind at His feet, she began to wash His feet, with tears, and wiped them with the hairs of her head, and kissed His feet, and anointed them with the ointment.

39. And the Pharisee, who had invited Him, seeing it, spoke within himself, saying: This man, if He were a prophet, would know . . that she is a sinner.

40. And Jesus answering, said to him: Simon, I have somewhat to say to thee. But he said: Master, say it.

41. A certain creditor had two debtors, the one owed five hundred pence, and the other

MARY MAGDALENE
Luke 8:2-3

2. And certain women who had been healed of evil spirits and infirmities; Mary who is called Magdalene, out of whom seven devils were gone forth.

3. And Joanna the wife of Chusa, Herod's steward, and Susanna, and many others who ministered unto him of their substance.

Matt. 27:55-61

55. And there were there many women afar off, who had followed Jesus from Galilee, ministering unto Him.

56. Among whom was Mary Magdalene, and Mary the mother of James and Joseph, and the mother of the sons of Zebedee.

57. And when it was evening, there came a certain rich man of Arimathea, named Joseph, who also himself was a disciple of Jesus.

58. He went to Pilate, and asked the body of Jesus. Then Pilate commanded that the body should be delivered.

MARY OF BETHANY
Luke 10:38-42

38. Now it came to pass as they went, that He entered into a certain town: and a certain woman named Martha received Him into her house.

39. And she had a sister called Mary, who sitting also at the Lord's feet, heard His word.

40. But Martha was busy about much serving. Who stood and said: Lord, hast Thou no care that my sister hath left me alone to serve? Speak to her therefore, that she help me.

41. And the Lord answering, said to her: Martha, Martha, thou art careful, and art troubled about many things:

42. But one thing is necessary. Mary hath chosen the best part, which shall not be taken away from her.

John 11:1-11

1. Now there was a certain man sick, named Lazarus, of Bethania, of the town of Mary and of Martha her sister.

2. (And Mary was she that anointed the Lord with ointment, and wiped His feet with

wherewith to pay, he forgave them both. Which therefore of the two loveth him most?

43. Simon answering, said: I suppose that he to whom he forgave most. And He said to him: Thou hast judged rightly.

44. And turning to the woman, He said unto Simon: Dost thou see this woman? I entered into thy house, thou gavest Me no water for My feet; but she with tears hath washed My feet, and with her hairs hath wiped them.

45. Thou gavest Me no kiss; but she, since she came in, hath not ceased to kiss My feet.

46. My head with oil thou didst not anoint; but she with ointment hath anointed My feet.

47. Wherefore I say to thee: Many sins are forgiven her, because she hath loved much. But to whom less is forgiven, he loveth less.

48. And He said to her: Thy sins are forgiven thee.

49. And they that sat at meat with Him began to say within themselves: Who is this that forgiveth sins also?

50. And He said to the woman: Thy faith hath made thee safe, go in peace.

wrapt it up in a clean linen cloth.

60. And laid it in his own new monument, which he had hewed out in a rock. And he rolled a great stone to the door of the monument, and went his way.

61. And there was there Mary Magdalene, and the other Mary sitting over against the sepulcher.

Matt. 28:1.

1. And in the end of the sabbath, when it began to dawn toward the first day of the week, came Mary Magdalene and the other Mary, to see the sepulcher.

John 20:18.

18. Mary Magdalene cometh, and telleth the disciples: I have seen the Lord, and these things He said to me.

Him, saying: Lord, behold, he whom Thou lovest is sick.

4. And Jesus hearing it, said to them: This sickness is not unto death, but for the glory of God: that the Son of God may be glorified by it.

5. Now Jesus loved Martha, and her sister Mary, and Lazarus.

6. When He had heard therefore that he was sick, He still remained in the same place two days.

7. Then after that, He said to His disciples: Let us go into Judea again.

8. The disciples say to Him: Rabbi, the Jews but now sought to stone Thee: and goest Thou thither again?

9. Jesus answered: Are there not twelve hours of the day? If a man walk in the day, he stumbleth not, because he seeth the light of this world:

10. But if he walk in the night, he stumbleth, because the light is not in him.

11. These things He said; and after that He said to them: Lazarus our friend sleepeth; but I go that I may awake him out of sleep.

In order to be able to make a better study of the Biblical accounts we shall divide them into three groups according as they deal with the sinful woman, Mary Magdalene, or Mary of Bethany. This is of the greatest importance in the investigation, and it may be well to state here, that nowhere in the writings of the Evangelists is there an interchange of names. Where the same event is narrated we never find a different name used in its parallel passages, and where the name Mary is used for both Mary Magdalene and Mary, Martha's sister, it is clear which of the two is meant in the parallel passages. This must be conceded even by those who wish to show the identity of persons from the Gospels. Were there only one Evangelist who uses Mary Magdalene or the "sinful woman" where the other Evangelist in the same context uses Mary, Martha's sister or Mary of Bethany, then our question would be answered.

Anyone who takes the pains to make a comparative study of this presentation of the various accounts must end by asking himself: How is it possible to come to the conclusion of uniting three persons who are separated by the Evangelists? The cause of this confusion is fourfold:

1. Luke 8:2 — "Mary who was called Magdalene, out of whom seven devils were gone forth." These words are taken to refer to the conversion of the one-time sinner and therefore Mary Magdalene is identified with her.

2. John 11:2 — "And Mary was she that anointed the Lord with ointment, and wiped His feet with her hair." Therein they say John denotes a woman who up to now has remained the anonymous sinner, who according to Luke 7:36 ff. anointed our Lord and dried His feet with

her hair. Thus the identification of the sinner with Mary of Bethany was completed, and through Luke 8:2 as a middle term, with Mary Magdalene, for two things equal to the same third are equal to each other.

3. The similarity of the anointing in the house of Simon the Pharisee (Luke 7:36 ff.) and in the house of Simon the Leper (Matt. 26:6 ff. and parallel passages) is the basis for identification. It seems improbable and incredible that two different women should anoint the Lord in such a similar manner, and use their hair for the same purpose.

4. The fourth argument for identification is found by the authors of this theory in the similar characters of Mary Magdalene and Mary of Bethany.

In this way arises the threefold identification: Mary Magdalene, the same as the sinful woman, who is identical with Mary of Bethany.

Let us examine each member of this identity separately.

A HARMONY OF THE GOSPEL MATERIAL

THE SINFUL WOMAN
Luke 7:36–50

Place: House of Simon the Pharisee in Capharnaum (according to some at Naim).

Time: Before the Galilean ministry (John 6:60–66), also in the second year of Christ's public life. Only Luke makes mention of this anointing by the sinful woman.

MARY MAGDALENE

Luke 8:2–3 — Mary Magdalene is called the first of the Galilean women who faithfully followed Jesus.

Matt. 27:55, 56 — Mary Magdalene is again mentioned as the first of the Galilean women under the cross. Parallel passages: Mark 15:40–41; Luke 23:49; John 19:25. (John mentions the Magdalene in the third place.)

Matt. 27:61 — Mary Magdalene at the burial. Cf. Mark 15:47; Luke 23:55.

Matt. 28:1 — Mary Magdalene goes to the sepulcher with the other women. Cf. Mark 16:1 ff.; Luke 24:1 ff.; John 20:1 ff. John speaks only of Mary Magdalene. She brings the news to Peter and John that the body is gone, hurries back to the tomb, where Jesus appears to her.

John 20:18 — Mary Magdalene (and acc. to Luke 24:9–10 the other women) announce the appearance of Jesus.

MARY OF BETHANY

Luke 10:38–42 — Mary, the sister of Martha sits at the feet of Jesus.
Place: From the context only Bethany near Jerusalem can be meant.

John 11:1–44 — Raising of Lazarus. Bethany is designated as the hamlet of Mary and her sister Martha. Then follows the important remark: "And Mary was she that anointed the Lord with ointment and wiped His feet with her hair."

Matt. 26:6–13 — Anointing of Jesus at Bethany in the house of Simon the Leper. Cf. Mark 14:3–9; John 12:1–8. Only John calls her Mary by name. The three reports are drawn from the same event which happened six days before the passion of Jesus. Jesus announces the fame of Mary to the murmuring disciples.

I. A HARMONY OF THE GOSPEL MATERIAL

In our modern editions of the New Testament a new chapter begins after Luke 7:50. Thereby the words of Luke 8:2, in the presentation to the reader, are unwittingly somewhat further removed from chapter 7. Let us call to mind the division into chapters and verses — both are, as is well known, later additions to the text — and if we read in one continued context Luke 7:36-8:4, we might probably think that the Evangelist wished to direct the remark of 8:2 to the same event which he previously narrated in full; or at least that he wished to show that Mary Magdalene was the same person who first appeared in the dining hall as a sinner.

Really, however, 8:1 begins a new section which depicts our Lord as the teacher of His disciples (8:1-11, 13). By it, we are informed in a summary way of the workings of Jesus with His companions in city and hamlet. The Evangelist makes a distinction among three groups: (1) the twelve Apostles; (2) "several women, who were cured of evil spirits and healed of sicknesses"; (3) "and many other women." The second and third groups are again connected: "Those who gave Him of their substance." Three representatives of the second group are mentioned specifically and in the first place, "Mary named Magdalene from whom seven demons were cast out."

27

Would St. Luke have acquainted us with this woman in such a detailed manner, if she were the same person whose tender love and deep contrition he had just described? Would he, who laid particular stress on stylistic and historical accuracy, present the same woman here as the constant follower of Jesus whom the Master just two verses before dismissed with the words: "Thy faith hath made thee safe; go in peace"?[1] Or did the Evangelist intentionally preserve a mysterious silence in order to shield the family of the one-time sinner, now a disciple, inasmuch as a clearer reference should have been painfully embarrassing? Does he, for the same reason, remain entirely silent concerning the name of the sinful woman in the preceding account? This explanation places too great an emphasis on the fact of the namelessness of the woman. It is a general rule that the person on whom Christ worked wonders of His power and grace remain unknown to us afterwards, unless there be some special reason for making him known.[2]

Dr. Urban Holzmeister, S.J., expressed the opinion

---

[1] ὕπαγε, or πορεύου εἰς εἰρήνην or ἐν εἰρήνη — was the oriental greeting at departing. Cf. Mark 5:34; Luke 8:48; Apoc. 16:36; James 2:16.

[2] Estius in a speech on the eve of the feast of Mary Magdalene 1609 said: "Cum enim septimo capite de peccatrice et poenitente muliere pertexit historiam [Lucas] nomen illius reticet, non ideo, quod quidam afferunt pro ratione, quia famae ejus honori consultum vellet. Quid enim ad consulendum ejus honori profuit, Evangelistam tacuisse nomen, si passim omnes per Ecclesiam fideles scituri erant, quaenam esset? Aut cur non eadem ratione Davidis et Petri nomen supressit Scriptura, quando eorum crimina nobis prodidit? Sed tacuit, quomodo aliorum atque etiam aliarum quae laudabiles fuere, nomina tacuerunt Evangelistae: velut illius Haemorrhoissae et Chananeae et illius quam hic idem Evangelista Lucas narrat extulisse vocem de turba atque dixisse Domino: Beatus venter qui te portavit et ubera quae suxisti." G. Estii Orationes theologicae (Venetiis: 1659), p. XXXVI.

that "the possibility is not entirely excluded, that the event in Luke 7 was related to him (Luke) without the name of the woman being mentioned, and he was not aware of her identity with the Magdalene. Hence he cannot be accused of an error any more than the author of the IV Book of Kings who, in 15:19 speaks of the Assyrian king Phul, and soon thereafter in 16:7 of Tiglath-Pileser without informing the reader that both names belong to the same person."[3] Admitting that the author of the IV Book of Kings knew nothing of the identity of the two names, the matter is considerably different in his case from that of the Evangelist Luke. The king really had two names, one Babylonian Phul, and another Assyrian Tiglath-Pileser. He united both kingdoms of Babylonia and Assyria under his own rule. It is, therefore, not at all extraordinary that at times he is mentioned under one name, and again at other times under his other name. Luke 7, however, makes no mention of the woman's name. Moreover, Luke did not write his Gospel about 200 years after the events narrated in chapters seven and eight, whereas the Books of the Kings were written about 560, while Phul reigned from 745-727. If the Evangelist had not known Mary Magdalene personally, he could have easily obtained information from those who knew as much of the sinful woman as of the much-spoken-of female disciple.

At the anointing at Bethany still less than here can the omission of the name by Matthew and Mark be explained because of regard for the family. The circumstances were so well known to the readers of the Gospels from preaching and catechizing that they could hardly

[3]*Biblica* 11, (1930), p. 465.

be concealed by the change of a name. If, however, no clearer data be given in Luke 8:2 on the past life of Mary Magdalene, out of regard for herself or for her brother or sister, then surely the actual additional characterization should have been suppressed in connection with the name Mary.

Commentators are quite generally agreed that the name Magdalene is derived from the place Magdala on the west bank of the Sea of Genesareth.[4] Julius Grill also employs this derivation in his work on historico-religious reconstructions, which shall be later referred to. There the opinion is expressed that Mary of Bethany had a landed estate, upon which she lived, separated from her family, and through her licentious life (association with Roman officers?) gained a bad reputation. Such is the firm belief of the defenders of the identity of the three women. Were that true, the Evangelist, by the surname Magdalene, should have hinted at Mary's past life, to which he did not directly allude out of regard for her family.

But actually the surname only shows that Mary, the disciple, who came from Magdala, is distinguished from the other Marys among Jesus' followers by the mentioning of her home.

By closer comparison of texts there arises a further difficulty against the identity of Mary Magdalene with the sinful woman: the woman, who, to the great horror

---

[4] We cannot prove that there was a place Magdala near Jerusalem which may be identical with Bethany. Lightfoot still leans to this opinion: *Horae hebr. et talmud.* in Luke 8:2; John 12:3. He also gives talmudic proof for the modern theory of the derivation of the name Magdalene from Magdala — hair artist (dresser); *Ibid.,* Matt. 27:56.

of the "pious" Pharisee interrupts the banquet, is known as a sinner in the city — ἐν τῇ πόλει. Therefore, she must have lived in the same city in which Simon the Pharisee had his home, i.e., most likely Capharnaum. We have placed the banquet there and not at Naim from the context of the account. That the sinner was of the same city as the guests'can be seen from the fact that the sinner is so well known (cf. Luke 7:39). If we accept that the three women are the same, the following constructions are necessary: (1) Mary Magdalene came from Bethany, where her sister and brother are still living; (2) she lived on her estate in Magdala, and for such a length of time that she became known as the Magdalene, the woman from Magdala; (3) at the time mentioned in Luke 7:36 ff., she no longer lived in Magdala, but in "the city" and there became known as a public sinner; Magdala, however, was no "city" but only a hamlet; (4) after John 11:1 she again lived long enough in Bethany so that this place is called her home, and only secondarily is noted as the home of her sister who always lived there — ἡ κώμη Μαρίας καὶ Μάρθας.

And the proof for this chain of hypotheses is exactly that which we must demonstrate through the hypotheses; namely, the identity of the three women.

If the chronology of Luke 8:1 ff. does not exactly correspond with that which goes before, there is no reason for the assumption of a long interval. The women mentioned in 8:2–3, since they are immediately placed next to the Apostles, must already have been, like the former, in the following of Christ for some time. The freeing of the Magdalene from the seven devils did not belong to the same epoch as Luke 7:36 ff. Furthermore we may not explain the phrase "from whom seven devils had gone forth," especially Luke's phrase, as a metaphorical signification of freeing from sin (7:48). Mark mentions the Magdalene as the woman "from whom He (Jesus) drove out seven demons" only in the history of the Resurrection (16:9). Nowhere in the New Testament are these words used to denote forgiveness of sin. We must further ask the reason why demoniacal obsession in the case of only the Magdalene is used in connection with a sinful life, since other women were also freed of evil spirits as is related in Luke 8:2. We should be led into serious difficulties if we should distort the unequivocal words of the Evangelist concerning the demoniacal obsession of the Magdalene and interpret them in a moral sense. Demoniacal possession and sin are essentially different concepts, and the power which the devil exercises over those possessed is altogether different from the influence which he exerts on the man who through sin has become a "slave of the evil one."[5]

Should we wish to assert that the Magdalene became possessed precisely because of her previous life of sin, and at the time of her healing was both possessed and a sinful woman, the event would be entirely possible although the assumption is not supported by any proof. And if on account of this assumption we identify the Magdalene with the sinful woman who anointed Jesus, we are guilty of a *petitio principii*. Only one thing would follow from this, that Mary Magdalene was also a sinner, but had nothing to do with the sinner at the banquet, since that woman was not possessed. Luke was a physician, and as such he was wont to make quite ac-

---

[5]Cf. Sickenberger, *Bibl. Zeitschr.* 17 (1925–26), pp. 67–68.

curate accounts of bodily and spiritual ills. Hence, when
he speaks of seven devils he must have had a real possession in mind, and also a specially serious case. But
from the scene in the house of Simon the Pharisee there
is nothing to show that the woman still suffered from
possession; in fact, everything seems to point to the opposite, if we compare the behavior of the sinful woman
with the conduct of the one possessed. In this Cardinal
von Faulhaber is agreed, because he views Luke 7:37–50
and 8:2 as two events separated in time, and places the
freeing of the Magdalene from the power of the demons
(8:2) before the appearance of the sinner at the banquet.
"The following scene (7:37 ff.) is to be viewed not as
the beginning, but as the conclusion of our Lord's act."[6]

The sinful woman is believed to have been freed of the
demons (8:2) in an earlier meeting with Jesus, "and with
all her energy which up to now she had used for evil,
she sought for an opportunity of thanking her Saviour.
This occasion presented itself in the home of Simon the
Pharisee, who on a certain day invited our Lord to dine
with him."[7] Though this hypothesis seems plausible, its
basis is not sound. While Faulhaber very decidedly declares, that "it is positively not allowed to hold that Mary
of Bethany and Mary Magdalene are one person, because
even their characters are entirely different,"[8] still he holds
the identity of the Magdalene with the sinful woman.
And yet, in the theory of identity of persons, the inverted
sequence of Luke 7:36 ff. and 8:2 is impossible. The clear

---

[6]Mich. von Faulhaber, "Charakterbilder der bibl. Frauenwelt," in
Charakterbilder der kathol. Frauenwelt, I, 1[8] (Paderborn, 1916),
p. 191.

[7]*Ibid.*

[8]*Op. cit.*, p. 197.

context of Luke 7:47–50 proves that the sinful woman first received forgiveness of her sins in the house of Simon the Pharisee. Would Jesus first have driven out the demons and still have left her in the bondage of sin? This would be contrary to His usual manner of acting. In His eyes, sin was the greater evil, which demanded healing first.[9] This does not demand that the sinner has met our Lord for the first time at the banquet. It is, on the contrary, very probable that the woman already had faith in the Messiah, acknowledged her need for mercy in the light of this faith, and felt her present condition so unbearable that without fear of human respect she sought forgiveness of her sins where it alone could be obtained. She had given public scandal and hence desired to give public evidence of her repentance and to seek remission. Not only gratitude, but especially true sorrow led her into the home of the Pharisee.

Still another reason against the identity of the sinful woman and Mary Magdalene can be drawn from the Evangelists: Mary Magdalene, together with Susanna and Joanna, belongs to that group of pious women who not only continually followed the Lord, but who supported Jesus and the Apostles by the giving of their substance (Luke 8:3). These women must have been of the well-to-do social class. This is especially true of Joanna, since she was the wife of Chusa, one of the officials in

---

[9]Cf. Luke 5:17–26: Healing of the man sick of the palsy. See Theod. Zahn, *Das Evangelium des Lukas* (Leipzig, 1913), pp. 324 ff. Zahn's interpretation of this passage asserts that Jesus did not forgive the guilt of the sins, but only wished to declare that God had already forgiven the sinful woman, and made this fact known to her through the words of Jesus. This explanation of Zahn is refuted by the clear text of Luke 7:49: "Who is this that also forgiveth sins?"

the court of Antipas. After the death of Jesus these same women purchase expensive spices with which to embalm His body. May we without a convincing argument admit that a woman of this class had been a noted public sinner of the city? When a woman is unreservedly called a sinner hardly anything can be meant but that she has sold her womanly honor for a price, as most of the Fathers interpret this passage. Without passing judgment on the inner moral condition of the various classes of society, it may be affirmed that as a rule girls and women from the lower strata become publicly known as sinners in this particular sense. Others at least preserve their external reputation.

In this last conception, the hypocritical and malicious conduct of the host is better illustrated. He was greatly provoked that a person of such a reputation should enter his honorable home. In his eyes she is not only marked with the stain of sin, but also belongs to the "Am ha-arez," with whom the "elect," the Pharisees, wished to have no intercourse. When H. Lesêtre assumes that the sinful woman must have belonged to the better class of society because a poor woman would not have been so well known in the city,[10] he transfers conditions of Paris to a provincial city of Palestine at the time of Christ.

That the sinful woman belonged to the "better classes of society" cannot be based on the assumption, that otherwise the domestics would have refused the woman admission.[11]

The host, being a Pharisee, in his narrow-mindedness

---

[10]See H. Lesêtre, "Marie Madeleine," in Vigouroux, *Dictionnaire de la Bible,* IV (Paris, 1908), pp. 809–18.

[11]See M. J. Lagrange, *Évangile selon Saint Luc* (Paris, 1921), p. 228.

was probably less led by moral considerations than by regard to his position and outward loyalty to the law as the Scriptural passage touching the adulteress makes known.

The reasons mentioned, if not singly, at least collectively ought to show that the identity of Mary Magdalene with the sinful woman is more than doubtful: it is exegetically untenable. If both are individual persons, then the strange hypothesis of K. Kastners on John 20:17, *"Noli me tangere,"* also fails. Why this rebuff of Jesus? According to Kastner's explanation, Mary, "once as a public sinner, committed sins against purity. Now the Lord appears to her in all the beauty of His glorified body. An approach to and touch of Him could call forth new temptations to her, in whom after the commission of so many sins there remained the fire of new lusts and inordinate desires. The Lord, therefore, who Himself had taught, 'lead us not into temptation,' wished to preserve His faithful and grateful disciple from such an occurrence."[12] Should the touching of the feet of the

---

[12] In *Bibl. Zeitschrift,* 13 (1915), pp. 351–52. The reply of Kastner to the difficulty of Röschs; in *Bibl. Zeitschrift,* 14 (1917), pp. 333–37, does not remove the doubt. See *Theol. u. Glaube* 9 (1917), pp. 651–52. Also the distinction between the objective and subjective working of Christ's body does not go to the heart of the question; just as little can perception of impure desires in holy persons of the feminine sex at the reception of Holy Communion be urged here. To be sure, the body of Christ is the same, but His mode of being is different, and that especially must be noted. It would be better to omit reference to the gardener in "relative nudeness," i.e., clothed only in a loin cloth, for the season of the year, the elevation of Jerusalem, and the early morning hour clearly speak against such an "attire," even if otherwise the gardeners of Palestine may have worn such a costume. On the eve of Easter it was still so cold that the soldiers made a fire even though they wore mantles. See Ketter, "Noli me tangere," in *Pastor bonus,* 31 (1918–19), pp. 272–77.

glorified Christ have been any more dangerous than the same act in the house of Simon? Should we not have to ascribe a high degree of hysteria or even mental disorder to the Magdalene, as is done by the Rationalists in order to weaken the witnesses of the Resurrection? Of Jesus we can say, and more so of the glorifed Christ, what Sollerius writes: "ea morum integritate fuisse (Christum), et tam casto aspectu, ut ne minima quidem impudicitiae suspicio vel in mentem cupiam venire potuerit."[18]

Now we shall examine the second member of the identity.

---

[18]See *Acta Sanctorum*, tom V. Julii, p. 195.

2. IS THE SINFUL WOMAN IDENTIFIED WITH MARY OF BETHANY?

It is not difficult to see where this identity arises; namely, as already stated, from John 11:2. The Evangelist wishes to narrate the great miracle of the raising of Lazarus, and therefore, in the first place, acquaints his readers with the main personages and their place of residence. This is done with a certain formality. It is striking that Bethany is not called "the hamlet of Lazarus," but "that of Mary and Martha, her sister." From verse one it is evident which of the various disciples named Mary is here meant, still the Evangelist devotes a whole verse to her distinguishing characteristic: ἦν δὲ Μαριὰμ ἡ ἀλείψασα τὸν κύριον μύρῳ καὶ ἐκμάξασα τοὺς πόδας αὐτοῦ ταῖς θριξὶν αὐτῆς.

Evidently John had a special purpose in mind. He is alluding to a well-known and oft-repeated event in the Christian assemblages. From the synoptic Gospels his readers already knew of two women who had anointed the Lord in the above-mentioned manner. They knew of two such anointings. The first is narrated in Luke 7:36 ff.; the other in Matt. 26:6 ff. and Mark 14:3 ff., but none of them mentioned the names of the women. To which of these anointings is John referring in 11:2? That is the kernel of our entire Biblical question. The text does not say directly, but a closer comparison of the text and context of John 11:2 makes it evident that reference is made to the anointing at Bethany, and not that in the house of Simon the Pharisee by the sinful woman.[14] John 11:2 should be definitive in our question only if the verse may be understood as referring to Luke 7:36 ff. So long as it can be referred to John 12:1 ff., it does not decide the matter.

According to the event as related in Luke 7:36 ff. the sinner first wet the feet of Jesus with her tears and then wiped them with her hair. Tears are mentioned twice (7:38 and 44) and thereupon she anointed the feet, as Jesus Himself declared (7:46). Whether she used her hair for wiping off the ointment Luke does not state. On the other hand, John 11:2 states that Mary anointed the Lord, i.e., first the head, and wiped the ointment from His feet with her hair. Nothing is said of tears which would have been particularly worthy of mention as a sign of repentance and love in a reference to Luke 7:36 ff. On the contrary, John 11:2 exactly corresponds to the narration of the anointing at Bethany according to John 12:3 ff. in connection with the parallel passages in Matt. 26:7; Mark 14:3. What the synoptics did not mention, namely, the anointing of the feet and the drying with the hair — they relate only the anointing of the head and the subsequent discourses — John supplies. In this instance it is again made clear that John presupposes the account of the older Evangelists, takes them into consideration, and supplements them according to necessity.

While the words of John 11:2 are easily understood

---

[14]*Die Indentität von Marias mit der Sünderin verteidigt auf Grund von Jo. 11:2;* also Leopold Fonck, S.J., in *Verbum Domini,* 8 (1928), pp. 65–74; 97–105.

as referring to the anointing at Bethany, they would be very obscure if referred in the context to the anointing by the sinful woman. Above all, they would in that case accomplish their main purpose only imperfectly, the purpose, namely, to better describe Mary and to distinguish her from the other disciple bearing the same name. In John 11:1 the readers are transported to Bethany, the hamlet of Mary and her sister Martha. To every reader of John's Gospel it was known through oral tradition and written data that shortly before our Lord's death, at this same hamlet, there had been a banquet in the home of Simon, the Leper, during which the Lord was anointed with costly ointment by a woman (γυνή). The Lord defended this woman against the murmuring of the disciples, especially of Judas, and even prophesied that her praise should be made known wherever· the Gospel be preached. By these words of Jesus the anointing at Bethany acquired a particular significance and distinction, much greater than the other one. But for the faithful of apostolic times it was simply regarded as an anointing of our Lord. Neither Mark nor Matthew give the name of the woman, not because of various family considerations, but because both insert the account by way of a supplement among the events in Jerusalem, and because neither of them had up to now mentioned anything concerning the relations of Jesus with the brother and sisters at Bethany. The fate of namelessness confused this woman in written documents with the sinful woman who once anointed the Lord in the house of Simon the Pharisee in a city the name of which is not given. Now John finds an opportunity for the first time to speak of Bethany, where an anointing took place. What would be easier, if the Evangelist wished in a special manner to distinguish Mary of Bethany — and that was his desire — than to point out that Mary was that woman among the other disciples of Jesus who bore that name, who anointed Him and wiped His feet with her hair? That he could have referred only to the anointing at Bethany was so evident from the context that he did not deem it necessary to give the name of the place again. What would have induced John to allude to the anointing by the nameless sinful woman as narrated by Luke? Would he then at least not have had to give the name of the place where that anointing took place? Or would he not have had to say: "Mary was that woman whose sins the Lord had forgiven, because she loved much"? That would have been a clear allusion to the sinful woman. The case would be different if both anointings had taken place in Bethany, as Lacordaire asserts, without solving the contradiction between John and Luke,[15] or if Luke had also given the name Mary to the sinner. John, however, first mentions the name Mary and then continues: "Mary was she that anointed the Lord with ointment, and wiped His feet with her hair." John 12:3 then takes this name for the woman who anointed the Lord. All these reasons urge us to accept John 11:2 as pointing not to Luke 7:36 ff., but to John 12:2 ff. and parallel passages. To designate John 11:2 as an old gloss, in default of proofs, is unwarranted. The identity, therefore, of the anonymous sinner with Mary of Bethany is in no way upheld in John; on the contrary it is indirectly disproved.

[15]See *Seele*, 7 (1925), p. 204.

There is still a weightier argument against the reference of John 11:2 to the anointing in Bethany which must not be overlooked. This is of a grammatical nature, based on the choice of the tenses. John chooses two aorist participles: ἀλείψασα, ἐκμάξασα. Now, if he meant the anointing at Bethany would he not have had to use words that refer to the future: μέλλουσα ἀλείφειν, or their equivalent since he will first treat of the anointing in the following chapter. All agree that the aorist must be used with reference to something past. But from the standpoint of the Evangelist as well as of the reader both anointings are past, and precisely because he is pointing to a known event he chose the past tense. The aorist participles need not be translated as pluperfects. Hence the Latin text has *unxit . . . extersit,* while a reference to Luke 7:36 ff. would rather demand the pluperfect. The best counterpart of this is found in Matt. 10:4, where long before the betrayal of Judas it was said: ὁ καὶ παραδοὺς αὐτόν, *qui et tradidit eum.* The parallel passages of Mark 3:19 and Luke 6:16 have the same past tense. Similarly John 4:44 — "Jesus Himself gave testimony (ἐμαρτύρησεν) that a prophet hath no honor in his own country." This declaration, however, was delivered only later, as the synoptics relate.[16] One cannot point to John 6:71 and 12:4 as a peculiar form of speech used by John in order to make John 11:2 refer to Luke 7:36 ff. Theod. Zahn correctly remarks concerning John 11:2: "The mention of the same [the anointing of Mary of Bethany] 11:2 cannot be compared to such references to an event which already happened and which has al-

---

[16]Matt. 13:57 and parall.

ready been narrated, like 4:46; 7:50; 10:40; 12:1; 19:29. According to its temporal form of expression it has not the meaning of a preliminary reference to a future occurrence which is to be related later,[17] but is a reminder of something known to the reader — a recollection belonging to the past both for the readers and for the Evangelists at the time of their writing. The only new material that John wishes to impart to his readers is simply this, that the woman who, as they know, once anointed the Lord and dried His feet with her hair is Mary, the sister of Lazarus and Martha, with whom the narration begun in 11:1 shall deal."[18] "The narration of Matt. 26:6-13; Mark 14:3-9 bears the same relation to the knowledge and lack of knowledge of the readers as Luke 10:42 bears to the form of expression of John 11:1. The setting according to Matt. and Mark is Bethany near Jerusalem; the time, a few days before our Lord's death."[19]

A further remark in the fourth Gospel found in the account of the raising of Lazarus gives us a new reason to deny the identity of the two women. From John 11:19, 31, 33, 37, 45, 46 we learn that many Jews from the neighborhood had come to Bethany to pay a visit to the mourning sisters. These Jews do not belong to the friends and disciples of Jesus. John would not have called such persons Ἰουδαῖοι five times in one chapter. With him this word usually has a political signification used to denote the followers of the Pharisees, the Jews, and the Pharisees

---

[17]Cf. 6:71; 7:39; 11:51; 12:4, 33; 18:32.

[18]See Theod. Zahn, *Das Evang. des Johannes*[3-4] (Leipzig, 1912), pp. 473-74.

[19]*Ibid.*, p. 474.

themselves.[20] These men again and again reproached the Lord for keeping company with sinners and visiting in their homes. If Mary of Bethany had been that woman described in Luke 7:37 and 39 as a sinner with whom Simon the Pharisee became angry because the Lord permitted Himself to be touched by such a woman, can we admit that these hypocritical Jews would soon afterwards have paid a friendly visit to the home of this woman? We need not hold that the same Pharisees and their friends were present at the banquet and at the tomb of Lazarus. Hypocrisy and external correct conduct were common to the entire sect.

But one could object that the sinful woman was converted, because Jesus forgave her sins. We grant that Mary was considered repentant, entirely changed in the eyes of Jesus and His disciples so that the Lord showed a special love for her (John 11:5) and visited with her family as a friend (Luke 10:38 ff.). For us that would be an example of divine love and mercy; but in the eyes of the Jews Mary would thereby be no more honored and no less despised. These haters of Jesus would have fled from the house of the one-time sinner. They had no faith in the power of Jesus to forgive sins. Only a part of them were converted through this incontestable miracle (John 11:45), while others became the Lord's accusers.

This argument from the conduct of the Jews appears to be stronger and clearer against the identity of the two women who anointed the Lord than the assertion that they cannot be the same person because Jesus out of respect for Himself and His disciples, would not have

---

[20]Cf. John 1:19; 2:18; 5:16, 18; 8:57, etc.

become so friendly with a person having such a past as the sinful woman. To support the latter argument we can turn to Luke 8:38–39; Mark 5:18–20, where the Lord did not permit the man whom He freed from unclean spirits to remain in His company. What the Lord meant by this prohibition we cannot exactly say. He alone must decide whom He wishes to have in His company, and we should go too far should we pass judgment as to how far Jesus might have gone in His love for the sinner.

Although the wording and the context of John 11:2 disprove the identification of Mary of Bethany with the sinful woman, many still deem it very improbable that two distinct women should have anointed the Lord in such a similar manner and used their hair to dry His feet.[21] This consideration moved some old and some modern commentators not only to consider the anointing women as identical but also both Simons, the hosts, and especially to identify the events related in Luke 7:36 ff., Matt. 26:6–13, and parallel passages. Others opposed to this were in favor of two or three anointings of Jesus in Bethany besides the one in the house of Simon the Pharisee in Galilee, because the chronology of the accounts of only one anointing in Bethany appears to be contradictory to them. Some of the Fathers, therefore, speak of three or four women who anointed Jesus, without, however, counting Mary Magdalene among them. Faillon, in his enthusiasm for the Provençal tradition,

---

[21]See Schuster-Holzammer, *Handbuch z. Bibl. Gesch.* II[8] (Freiburg, 1926), pp. 217–18. The revision by J. Schäfer still supports the reasons for the identity of person alleged by Le Camus. It is worthy of note, however, that the heading of the section is no longer "Die Büsserin Magdalena" [the penitent Magdalene] but "Die ungenannte Sünderin und Büsserin" [the anonymous sinner and penitent].

goes so far as to place under theological censure those who refuse to hold with him that Jesus was only anointed once by one woman at a banquet.[22] And yet, without a doubt, we must distinguish between Luke 7:36 ff. and John 12:1 ff., and the same event contained in the latter text is also narrated in Matt. 26:6–13 and Mark 14:3–9. The seeming contradictions between the accounts concerning the time and place are easily solved. According to John it need not be admitted that the banquet was given in the house of the brother and two sisters, while Matt. and Mark misplace it in the house of Simon the Leper.[23] The mere conjecture, devoid of proofs, which Theophylactus records as an opinion of one sole author, may be noticed, viz.: that this Simon be the dead father of Lazarus, Mary, and Martha.[24] After the death of the father, Martha, the elder of the two daughters, managed the affairs of the home. And as it often happens in similar instances, the house would sometimes be known after its former master (Matt. 26:6; Mark 14:3); sometimes after its present mistress (Luke 10:38). John 12:2 seems to go against this belief, for John states that Lazarus was one of those who sat at table with Jesus; which need not be mentioned had the event taken place in his own home.[25] The opinion is not made valueless by this consideration since the Evangelist by this remark wishes to show that Lazarus, after his restoration to life, ate and drank like other men. Lazarus must have been

---

[22]See M. Faillon, *Monuments inédits*, I, p. 64.

[23]See Knabenbauer, *Comment. in Matthaeum*, II, p. 393.

[24]See Schanz, *Comment. über d. Ev. d. hl. Matth.*, p. 504.

[25]See L. Fonck, "Cena Bethanica," in: *Verbum Domini*, 8 (1928), p. 70.

much younger than his sisters, and in ill health, otherwise it would have been his duty to direct the household. Martha is always presented to us as a resolute, practically gifted woman, who must constantly see that everything is done properly, and cannot reconcile the conduct of the more contemplative life of her sister Mary. Were Jesus anointed only once by one woman, the event would have had to take place either in Galilee or in Bethany. In the first case, the time of John 12:1 would be false because the anointing would have to come before the raising of Lazarus. In the second instance the sinful woman would have first been converted in Bethany which is incompatible with Luke 8:2-3 and 10:38-42.

In view of the foregoing considerations, we have accepted two anointings of Jesus at a banquet. Are both anointings so similar that only one and the same woman could have performed them? The similarities and dissimilarities in the accounts stand out more clearly by a comparison of the most important declarations of each of the Evangelists.

ANOINTING BY THE SINFUL WOMAN

Luke 7:36 ff. — A Pharisee invited Jesus to eat with him. He entered the house of the Pharisee and sat down at table. There was a woman who was known in the city as a sinner. When she learned that Jesus was a guest in the house of the Pharisee, she brought an alabaster box of ointment and approached His feet from behind. She began to weep, washing His feet with her tears and drying them with her hair. Then she kissed His feet and anointed them with the ointment. The Pharisee who invited Him, seeing this, said within himself: Were this man a prophet He would know who and what kind of woman this is who toucheth Him.

She is a sinner. Jesus says to her: "Thy sins are forgiven thee." The other guests begin to say within themselves: Who is this that forgiveth sins? He said to the woman: "Thy faith hath saved thee; go in peace."

ANOINTING BY MARY OF BETHANY

Matt. 26:6 ff. — As Jesus tarried in the house of Simon the Leper in Bethany a woman approached Him with an alabaster box of ointment and anointed His head while He was reclining at table. When the disciples saw this they said indignantly: "Why this extravagance? This could be sold and the money given to the poor." Jesus observing them said to them: "Why do ye molest this woman? She has wrought a good work upon Me. The poor ye have always with you, but Me ye have not always. For she in pouring this ointment upon My body hath done it for My burial. Amen I say to you, wheresoever this gospel shall be preached in the whole world, that also which she hath done, shall be told for a memory of her."

Mark 14:3 ff. — When he was in Bethany in the house of Simon the Leper and sat at meat, there came a woman having an alabaster box of ointment of precious spikenard: and breaking the box, she poured it out upon His head. Some that had indignation within themselves said: Why was this waste of ointment made? This ointment might have been sold for more than 300 pence and given to the

her. But Jesus said: "Let her alone. Why do ye molest her? She hath wrought a good work upon Me. . . . She hath done what she could: she is come beforehand to anoint My body for the burial. Amen I say to you . . ." (same as Matt. 26:13).

John 12:1 ff. — Six days before the Pasch, Jesus came to Bethany where Lazarus was, whom Jesus raised to life. And they made Him a supper and Martha served: but Lazarus was one of them that sat at table with Him. Mary, therefore, took a pound of ointment of spikenard, of great value, and anointed the feet of Jesus, and wiped them with her hair, and the house was filled with the odor of the ointment. Then one of the disciples, Judas Iscariot, he that was about to betray Him, said: "Why was not this ointment sold for 300 pence and given to the poor?" Now he said this not because he cared for the poor but because he was a thief, and having the purse, carried what was put therein. But Jesus said: "Let her alone, that she may keep it against the day of My burial. For the poor ye have always with you: but Me ye have not always."

accounts, the following dissimilarities still remain:

ANOINTING BY THE SINNER

1. PLACE AND TIME: In Galilee, before the second-last Passover.
2. THE HOST: Simon the Pharisee.
3. THE PERSON ANOINTING: An anonymous sinner, at whose appearance the Pharisee is greatly vexed. She was not invited.
4. MOTIVE FOR ANOINTING: Repentance and gratitude for being freed from the guilt and disgrace of sin.
5. MANNER OF ANOINTING: First wetting of the feet with tears of sorrow, wiping of the feet with hair, then kissing and anointing of only the feet, as related in Luke 7:46.
6. KIND OF OINTMENT: No special description of the ointment.
7. CONCLUSION OF THE SCENE: The sinful woman is dismissed by Jesus in peace.

ANOINTING BY MARY OF BETHANY

1. In Judea, six days before the passion.
2. Simon the Leper.
3. Mary who takes part in the banquet, and herself is an intimate friend of Jesus. She belongs to a rich and respected family, as proved by the frequent visits of condolence from Jerusalem and the cost of the ointment.
4. Honor to the guest, gratitude for the raising to life of her brother, loving consecration of the last reunion in anticipation of the anointing after death.
5. Pouring of precious ointment on the head; afterward the anointing of the feet and wiping thereof with her hair, not of tears, but of the ointment.
6. Spikenard, whose costliness is mentioned by the three Evangelists, and gives occasion for complaint of waste.
7. Mary remains at the meal and Jesus prophesies her renown.

One could also point out the entirely different impressions of the scenes upon those present. The following are common: (1) Both hosts have the name Simon. (2) Both women anoint Jesus during the meal, and have the ointment in an alabaster box. (3) Both dry the feet of Jesus with their hair.

The same name does not give the least reason why the two hosts should be identified. Suffice it to say that in the New Testament there are nine different Simons (and four Simeons), and that Flavius Josephus mentions twenty of them living in the same century. Simon is the most frequently occurring name among the men. Schürer, in his register, mentions eight priests bearing the name Simon, eight Rabbis, and eight other men. That in both accounts an alabaster box is mentioned does not justify a further conclusion. Αλάβαστρος is used in the sense of our "glass," as a vessel and at the same time a measure. John 12:3 uses also λίτραν, pound.[26] Only the anointing and the drying of the feet with the hair, in the first case of the tears, in the second of the ointment, still remain as striking similarities. The following historical considerations take away from the two women's manner of acting much which seems extraordinary in our times:

The anointing of the head at a meal was an old custom.[27] It was considered a duty of courtesy toward distinguished guests.[28] The ointment was not used sparingly

---

[26] Cp. our "glass of water."

[27] Cf. Ps. 22:5; 44:8. The use of ointment belonged to the care of the body: Eccles. 9:8; Amos 6:6; Ezech. 19:9; Ruth 3:3; Matt. 6:17; II Sam. 12:20.

[28] See Luke 7:46.

according to Ps. 133 (132) :2. A gloss of the Babylonian Talmud mentions this custom as a special sign of honor to learned doctors of the law.[29] The kissing of the feet seldom took place. It was considered dishonorable among the Greeks and Romans, but came to be used by the Jews as a sign of respect and gratitude.[30] The washing of the feet was mostly done by servants, but as a mark of special honor it was performed by the mistress.[31]

The use of the hair for drying the feet may be explained in several ways: it is to be noted that the anointing at Bethany certainly took place on a sabbath, as did probably also that by the sinful woman. The Jews were wont to have their solemn banquets on that day. Even the poor should partake of a better meal on the sabbath, if possible with a little wine. Everyone is acquainted with the regulations touching the sabbath-rest on which even at the time of Christ special emphasis was placed by the doctors of the law. The hair-dressing of women was included under this ruling. It is not difficult to assume that the two women who anointed the Lord had long, flowing hair. Then the use of the hair in drying the feet of Jesus, over which they were bent, becomes

---

[29]See Lightfoot, *Horae hebr. et talmud.*, in Mark 14:3. To permit such an honor to be shown toward one seemed to many to be a mark of effeminacy, and Lightfoot conjectures that it was for this reason that the disciples murmured against the anointing. Whether this conjecture is true remains uncertain. At a wedding of a woman it was customary in Babylon that the head of the Rabbis present be anointed by women. As soon as this had taken place the news was brought to the respective bride. Cf. Strack-Billerdeck, *Kommentar zum Neuen Test. aus Talmud und Midrasch*, I (München, 1922), pp. 427, 986. On the Kissing of the Feet, *Ibid.*, p. 96.

[30]Lightfoot, *op. cit.*, in Matt. 28:9; Mark 10:17.

[31]See I Tim. 5:10.

more comprehensible and less surprising than if the hair had first to be let down. It is especially interesting to note here another gloss of the Talmud concerning the conduct of a woman who administered oil to a sick person without breaking the sabbath-rest: she must use her hair, "atque per hanc actionem non violat Sabbatum."[32] Even if in the above example the bearing of the box of ointment should be avoided on the sabbath, since two women at the anointing of the Lord carried the box in their hand, the talmudic gloss casts some light on the use of the hair. To the things with which a woman could not go out on the sabbath belongs the covering worn over the hair.[33] The fact is related that Mirjam, the daughter of Nakdemon ben Gorjon, a contemporary of Jesus, appeared before the renowned Rabban Jochanan ben Zakkai with flowing hair.[34] None of the Evangelists mention that the anointing women's manner of acting was in any way strange. In the first case, the criticism centers upon the character of the woman as a sinner; in the second, upon the costliness of the ointment.

Apart from the consideration of the day of the week and the regulations of the sabbath, the conduct of both women is not so amazing as it appears to us. J. Leipoldt declares: "To me the differences of both accounts of the anointings are so great that I could not combine them into one event. They will not appear as a duplication to one who knows the customs of the ancients: anointing and washing of the feet play a great rôle in invitations."[35]

---

[32]See Lightfoot, *op. cit.*, in John 12:3.
[33]See Strack-Billerdeck, *op. cit.*, III, p. 432.
[34]See Strack-Billerdeck, *op. cit.*, II, pp. 414–15.
[35]J. Leipoldt, *Jesus und die Frauen* (Leipzig, 1921), p. 130.

Egyptian pictures portray mourning women from Syria with flowing hair. On the sarcophagus of Achiram of Byblos, mourning women have their hair loose, hanging over the shoulders.[36] The tears of sorrow of the sinful woman and the anointing of Jesus "for the burial" by Mary of Bethany raise the question whether both women considered themselves as mourning, and hence wore their hair loose? A domestic at a meal is represented in a fresco in the Peter Marcellinus Catacomb in Rome with loose-flowing hair.[37] The miniature of the banquet at Bethany found in Trierer Egbert-Kodex seems to go back to the oldest originals, for both Mary and Martha have flowing hair.

According to the scanty accounts which we possess, the action of the women who anointed the Lord appears as something uncommon. For their contemporaries it was not considered as such.

But let us for once admit that the event was very extraordinary. Just on that account we need not hold to the identity of both women. There is still another explanation which was already mentioned by Theophylact.[38]

Between the event in the house of Simon the Pharisee and the farewell banquet in Bethany, there is a long interval. If the manner and method by which the one-time sinner showed her love and gratitude to the Lord had been something unusual for her contemporaries, the event should have been spoken of more, especially in

---

[36]J. Benzinger, *Hebräische Archäologie*[2] (Leipzig, 1927), p. 94, and illustration 53.

[37]H. Achelis, "Altchristliche Kunst," in *Zeitschr. f. d. neutest. Wiss.*, 17 (1916), plate III.

[38]Migne, *P. gr.* 123, 793. Also Theod. Zahn, *Das Evan. des Lukas*, p. 335.

the circle of our Lord's disciples. From the words of Jesus spoken to the host, Simon, all knew how pleasing this manifestation of grateful love was to the heart of the Master. And now the Lord sits at a banquet in Bethany. Shortly before He had given a wonderful proof of His love for the two sisters, Mary and Martha, by raising their brother Lazarus to life. They wish to show their love in return, each in a manner befitting her character. Martha serves the meal. Mary, however, thought of a personal way in which to honor and rejoice the Lord; namely, to anoint Him and dry His feet with her hair as had already been done at a banquet. Still another motive urged her on. She knew that in the next few days the dread catastrophe should fall upon the beloved Master, that His enemies were already plotting against Him, and that His death was inevitably very near. Therefore, she is intent upon giving a loving consecration to this farewell banquet, which at the same time points to the imminent burial of Jesus. The Saviour Himself later refers to this event. Mary uses costly spikenard for the anointing, and even if she imitates the example of the other woman who previously honored and gladdened the Lord by her anointing, she avoids everything which in her entirely different circumstances would be unsuitable to Him. Thus the similarities and differences of the two anointings of Jesus are easily explained.

It is very noteworthy that only Luke gives us the touching scene of repentance in the house of Simon the Pharisee, and he alone mentions nothing of the anointing in Bethany. Luke depicts the Lord with preference as the Friend and Saviour of the poor, of the despised sinner. Only from him do we learn the sublime parable of the publican and the pharisee (18:9–14), of the poor guests (14:12–14), of the Good Samaritan (10:30–37), of the lost drachma (15:8–10), of the Prodigal Son (15:11–22). In Luke alone we find the comforting sentence that there is more joy in heaven over one sinner that does penance, than over ninety-nine righteous who need not penance (Luke 15:7); only Luke mentions the visit of Jesus with Zachaeus the publican (19:1–10). Had Luke known the sinful woman also as Mary of Bethany, and that would have been necessary if both persons were the same, he would have found in the account of the anointing at Bethany a new and wonderful example of the pardoning love of Jesus for the sinner which he could scarcely have left unmentioned. In his account (10:38–42) of the visit of Jesus at Bethany with the brother and sisters, Luke likewise nowhere points to a former life of sin in the contemplative character of Mary.

3. IS MARY MAGDALENE THE SAME AS
MARY OF BETHANY?

The Evangelists do not identify the two women, even though both bear the name Mary. This is to be especially noted in John. He is very careful with the designation of persons, if some confusion is apt to arise (cf. 11:16; 14:22). He differentiates four Marys by some addition to the name Mary. Never does he write: Mary, the sister of Lazarus, who is also called Magdalene, or Mary Magdalene, the sister of Martha, or Mary the converted sinner, where not only a confusion might arise, but where especially today we find so much trouble.[39] The fourth Evangelist should have led his readers into error if Mary, the sister of Lazarus, and Mary Magdalene be one person. John, as a participant in the banquet at Bethany, alone gives us the name of the woman who anointed Jesus. As an eyewitness (in 19:25) he distinguishes among three Marys under the cross, and this by a special addition to their names. Through this fact the name Mary Magdalene appears for the first time in his gospel.

Mary Magdalene is the most frequently mentioned of the three women under consideration — in all not less than fourteen times. Would it not be surprising that not once is there an allusion to her relationship with Martha and Lazarus, or to her home in Bethany, if she really

---

[39] See Knabenbauer, *Comment. in Matth.* II, p. 400.

were Mary of Bethany? The identification of other persons having various names is not difficult, even though the use of names is interchanged: Simon — Peter — Cephas; Matthew — Levi; Nathanael — Bartholomew. Frequent interchange of these names is found, especially in their use by our Lord Himself. That a similar exchange in the use of the various designations Mary Magdalene, Mary, the sister of Martha, or of Lazarus, does not occur, is not to be explained only in deference to the family; certainly this regard would not prevail everywhere and would not have been used by John around the year 90. And what is so defamatory about Mary Magdalene in the New Testament that men should wish to pass it by in silence? That she was freed from demoniacal possession? The wife of Chusa was also freed from demons without any concealment of the distinguished position of her husband. We must not fall into the vicious circle of first uniting in one person the different names recorded by the Evangelists, and then assigning as the reason for the choice of the various designations regard for the family. If the two Marys or all three women are identical, why, for example, does Luke in 10:38 introduce Mary of Bethany to his readers as a person up to this point entirely unknown? He himself has already spoken of Mary Magdalene (8:2) and made her known to us, and has already related the conversion of the sinful woman. Why, then, in 10:38 does he again choose an entirely different characteristic and specification of the oft-repeated name Mary as he did in 8:2? In the one account she is a depraved city woman; in the other, a worthy, pious woman of the hamlet Bethany. We cannot accept without cogent reasons such inequalities of representation, least of all in the cultured and historically accurate Evangelist, St. Luke.

Just as the Evangelists are consistent in their use of distinguishing additions to the names of both Mary Magdalene and Mary of Bethany, so also the character portrayal of each is faithfully drawn by all of them. Mary of Bethany is depicted as the reserved, contemplative soul, whom we see out of the house only once and that at the tomb of her brother; and even then she must be summoned (John 11:28, 31). She listens eagerly to the words of Jesus, and for that reason forgets to lend help to her sister (Luke 10:39 ff.). At the death of her brother she remains in the house weeping, and is made aware of the Lord's coming by Martha. At the greeting of Jesus she repeats word for word what Martha had said. At the tomb she remains in silent sorrow. At the solemn banquet at Bethany she leaves the serving to Martha. Mary is just the opposite of Martha, the practically minded mistress of the house, who considers it her duty to serve a well-prepared meal to her guests (Luke 10:40), who realizes that even in time of great grief someone must take care of the household (John 11:20), and who is intent upon removing a disagreeable experience from the Lord at the grave of her brother (John 11:39).

Let us now compare the Biblical account of Mary Magdalene with the character description of Martha's sister. While the latter is satisfied with greeting the Lord in her home, there to listen to His words, the former, like a true disciple, follows Him from place to place administering with her substance to the wants of Jesus and

His Apostles (Luke 8:3). She remains beneath the cross and after the death of her Master does not remain behind closed doors, but is even present at the sepulcher. As soon as the sabbath-rest is over, she hurries on that first Easter morn to the sepulcher, there to embalm the body (Mark 15:47; Matt. 28:1 ff.). Finding the tomb empty, she considers it her duty first to inform Peter and John (John 20:1 ff.); then she hurries back to the sepulcher intent upon personal investigation as to where the body may be, and, if need be, to take it away herself (John 20:15). This bespeaks such a stamped practical outlook and such social experience that Mary Magdalene in her characteristics is rather more like Martha than her sister Mary. John Weiss builds up the approach to an understanding of the Magdalene's character when he writes on Mark 16:1 ff: "Furthermore it is very noteworthy, and one will hardly doubt that John 20 mentions the fact that on the dawn of Easter morn Mary Magdalene was deeply concerned that something might have befallen her beloved Master. The event is related not of the three women, but only of Mary Magdalene (Luke 8:2) since John may have inclined more particularly to such events."[40] Why does Weiss place more emphasis on the account that Mary Magdalene was possessed by seven demons (according to him she was diseased) than on the express mention of her healing? Nowhere do we find the slightest trace of her relapse into her former state. There is no justification for the assertion that "exorcism had to be repeated on Mary Magdalene; for her own part she remained close to

[40]See John Weiss, *Die Schriften des N.T.*, I², p. 226.

Jesus because from Him she sought and found cure and protection for herself."[41] She remained always near Jesus after she had been cured by Him, and that out of gratitude and to help His cause by her co-operation.

Just as the diversity of home conditions of the two women creates a strong argument against the identity of Mary Magdalene and the sinful woman, a greater argument opposes the identification of Mary Magdalene and Mary of Bethany. The alibi proof may also be used here.

Of Mary Magdalene it is repeatedly related that she belonged to the "women of Galilee" in whose company we always find her. She is found alone only once, and that is at the tomb where she remained after the departure of those who accompanied her; or better, after she returned a second time. She belongs to the faithful followers of Jesus in the specific sense of the word. Just the opposite is true of Mary of Bethany whom we meet, as already remarked above, only once out of her home, and never beyond the limits of the hamlet where she lived. Another series of combinations is necessary, therefore, in order to explain the various accounts of Mary Magdalene and the sister of Martha as referring to one and the same person, combinations whose point of departure is similar to that which was necessary for the unproved identity of Mary of Bethany with the sinful woman. After Luke

---

[41] John Weiss, *loc. cit.*, 1^2, p. 81. It is very characteristic that here greater historical reliability is given to the Gospel of St. John than to the synoptics, while at other times the credibility of this Gospel is valued as unimportant by Weiss. The inner experiences of the disciples are more difficult to explain in the synoptic accounts.

(8:1-3) expressly states that Mary Magdalene followed the Lord from Galilee through the cities and towns, he mentions in his "account of the travels": "Now it came to pass, as they went, that He entered into a certain town, and a certain woman named Martha received Him into her house: And she had a sister, who sitting also at the Lord's feet, heard His word" (Luke 10:38). Who would think that this sister of Martha to whom we are here introduced as for the first time, has really been one of the followers of Jesus ever since His departure from Galilee, one of those who ministered to the Lord on the way (Luke 8:3), yet now (10:38) is suddenly no longer a woman from Galilee, but lives with her sister in Bethany where she awaits the Lord, not to minister unto Him as she had done heretofore, but devoutly to recline at His feet, in order to grasp every word attentively as one who seldom enjoyed this privilege? The somewhat indignant remark of Martha concerning Mary's conduct and the answer of Jesus would be much more difficult to understand than it already is, if Mary had come with Jesus to Bethany.

According to John 11:1 ff. Martha's sister also remained at Bethany. There she anoints our Lord shortly before His death. In the beginning of the week of our Lord's passion, Jesus betakes Himself at nightfall to the house of the faithful sisters and brother, and in the morning again returns to Jerusalem. At the crucifixion, as related by the synoptics (Matt. 27:55 ff.; Mark 15:40 f.; Luke 23:49; cf. John 19:25), several women are present among whom Mary Magdalene is mentioned first by Matthew and Mark. Then both Evangelists remark that these women became associated with Jesus while he was in Galilee, that she and many others ministered unto Him and came up with Him to Jerusalem. What Luke has previously mentioned (8:1–3) and what he repeats (23:49) without stating the name, Matthew and Mark take up, from which it is clear that Mary Magdalene in the interval between Luke 8:1–3 and the passion was in the company of Jesus, and hence cannot be identified with Martha's sister who remained in Bethany. This conclusion is strengthened by the fact that the mother of the sons of Zebedee is mentioned among the Galilean women on Golgotha and at the tomb of Jesus next to Mary Magdalene (Matt. 27:56; Mark 16:1). During the same period this mother is also found in the company of Jesus.

Furthermore, if Mary Magdalene be the same person as Mary of Bethany, she most probably would have returned to Bethany situated close by on the eve following Christ's death, and we should not meet her again immediately on Friday evening just before the beginning of the sabbath-rest, and again on Sunday morning "while it was still dark" in Jerusalem and in the company of the women from Galilee as one of them. At the sepulcher the angel says to her: "Remember how He spoke to you, when He was yet in Galilee, saying: The Son of man must be delivered into the hands of sinful men, and be crucified, and the third day rise again. And they remembered His words" (Luke 24:6–8). When had Jesus spoken these words? They are found in Matt. 17:22–23; Mark 9:31; Luke 9:44. At that time also Mary Magdalene was with Jesus in Galilee and not in Bethany, where we meet the sister of Martha for the first time as already related by Luke in 10:38.[42]

James Schäfer, following Le Camus, finds it strange that "nothing is said concerning the soul so faithful, loyal, and dear to the Lord (Mary of Bethany) in the great scenes of the Lord's passion and resurrection, and that she did not have the strength to finish her noble act of the embalming of Jesus, which she had begun with such determination while He was still alive."[43] This causes him to identify the two women. In answer to this objection we may say that Lazarus and Martha were also faithful and loyal friends of the Lord[44] and still they are not mentioned either at the passion, or at the resurrection of Jesus. Whether or not they were actually in Jerusalem with their sister Mary on Good Friday, and returned to their home before the sabbath cannot be known with certainty because of the silence of the Evangelists. The brother and sisters of Bethany had a strong reason for remaining away from Jerusalem, for John 12:10 relates that the death sentence of the Sanhedrin was passed on Lazarus. The Evangelists say nothing to advise us that Jesus first appeared to His Mother on Easter morning, and yet we can take it for granted, because His Mother would surely also have hurried to the tomb.

---

[42]The argument is also valid if Mary Magdalene immediately upon seeing the empty tomb hurried back to the city; for the words of the angel are directed to the women of Galilee, in whose company we always find the Magdalene, for she was the one who led the group out to the sepulcher.

[43]See *Handbuch z. Bibl. Geschichte*, II[8], p. 218.

[44]See John 11:3, 5, 36.

The words spoken by Jesus at His anointing in Bethany can be understood only if this anointing at the supper was not performed by Mary Magdalene. Jesus defends Mary's action against the murmurings of the disciples, and says: "She hath done what she could. She hath anointed aforehand My Body for the burial" (Mark 14:8). This can only be explained as signifying that Mary of Bethany after the Lord's death would have no opportunity to anoint the body of her Master, and hence anticipated this demonstration of Love. Mary Magdalene, however, took part in the anointing of the body. To her Jesus could not have said that she did by the anointing in Bethany that which she was able to do. The correct explanation of the parallel text of John 12:7 proves the same point. He cannot say: "Let her alone so that she may keep it against the day of My burial," because a preserving of the spikenard which was already used up was no longer possible. The cruse was broken (Mark 14:3), most probably by thrusting through the thin bottom, as may be seen in many representations in sepulchers. Τηρήση in this passage does not mean to preserve, *conservare,* but to use, employ, *observare;* hence, "Let her alone, so that she may employ it for the day of My burial" — that she may do now what will be impossible for her to do later on.[45]

Having examined the above considerations, we can conclude without any exaggeration that the gospel narratives speak for the non-identification of the three women, and oppose their identification. With a slight touch of sarcasm, Calmet cites the confession of Pezro-

---

[45]See G. Wohlenberg, *Das Evangelium des Markus,* p. 343.

nius, a decided defender of the identity: "Ex rerum, quae de Magdalena in Evangelio narrantur, historia, si sparsim, uti scriptis mandata est, legitur, non nisi confusam ejus notitiam esse orituram; si vero junctim tamquam in ordinatae historiae seriem digesta exhibeatur, tunc prona erunt omnia et aperta."[46] To this Calmet remarks: "Quam invidiosam illius systematis confessionem! Quae in Evangelio res gestae leguntur, nullam habent ad persuadendum vim, nisi e suo revulsae loco in arbitrariam seriem reducantur: quid tunc alienum erit ab Evangelio, si ea tandem interpretandi ratio adhibeatur?"[47] With this, Calmet lays bare the most vulnerable element in the system of the identification of the three women. The defenders of this system proceed with a preconceived plan in explaining this identity. The unproved identity of persons is the starting point and the aim at the same time. Without this presupposition, however, nothing can be found in the Gospels that points to the fact that the various names refer to the same person.

---

[46]See Calmet, *Dissertationes in Vet. et Nov. Test.*, III (Wirceburgi, 1789), p. 182.
[47]*Ibid.*

II. TRADITION

Were we face to face with a unanimous tradition of
the Fathers and older theologians concerning the explanations of the Biblical accounts dealing with the sinful
woman, Mary Magdalene, and Mary of Bethany, then
our question would be easy to decide. We should then
have to admit that the Fathers, especially those of the
earliest period, had in their possession historical sources
and possibilities of orientation to which we have no
access today. Even though the historico-critical method
was unknown to them as such, their interest in the truth
was just as great as ours. But when we examine the views
of the Fathers on the question of the Magdalene, we
are confronted with a veritable confusion of opinions.
In the Latin Church, especially during the Middle Ages
and in modern times, the assumption of the identity of
the three women found more approbation. One who
knows the great influence of Gregory the Great on Biblical explanations of the Middle Ages will not wonder
at this, for it is precisely in his homilies that Gregory
stands for their identity. And yet even the great authority of a St. Gregory did not entirely impose silence upon
the opponents of the identity during the Middle Ages.
As soon as the "golden age of exegesis" set in in Catholic
circles in the sixteenth and seventeenth centuries, more

and more voices were raised for the distinction of the three women. And therefore, when French defenders of the Provençal tradition with bias appeal to the witnesses who followed Gregory the Great, they must be reminded that: "Testes non sunt numerandi sed ponderandi." The independence of these later witnesses is, moreover, at times so evidently weak that they borrow entire pages of their material without mentioning their sources.

J. M. Lagrange made a thorough study of the patristic tradition concerning the women who anointed the Lord. Therefore he could employ texts which up to now were either unknown or disregarded, and he arrives at the following conclusion: "Ils sont point d'accord, et presque aucun n'est très affirmatif. Ce qui est plus étrange, c'est qu' aucun d'eux, aucun, n'ait fait appel à un souvenir traditional qu'on aurait conservé ici ou là de la ou des myrophores. . . . Il n'existe dont pas plus chez les Pères de tradition historique que de tradition exégétique. . . . Ainsi les exégètes ou ne concluent pas(ou concluent que la pécheresse n'est pas Marie de Béthanie, tandis que tous les prédicateurs, même ceux qui pensaient autrement comme exégètes (Ephrem, Jérôme comme allégoriste) n'ont pas cessé de supposer l'unité. Et c'est eut qui l'ont emporté."[1]

_____

[1] "They are not of accord, and scarcely one makes a positive affirmation. That which is more strange is that no one among them appeals to a tradition preserved there of her or of the anointers. . . . There is among the Fathers neither a historical nor an exegetical tradition. . . . Also the exegetes either draw no conclusion, or declare that the sinful woman is not Mary of Bethany, at the same time that all the preachers, even those who as exegetes think otherwise (Ephrem, and Jerome, the allegorist) consistently identify and rhetorically exploit this identity." See: _Jésus a-t-il été oint plusieurs fois et par plusieurs femmes?_ in _Revue Biblique:_ New Series, 9 (1912), pp. 504–532.

The various Biblical passages can be used to greater advantage homiletically and ascetically, if they are united into one account and applied to only one woman. And Lagrange is correct when he asserts that herein lies the ultimate reason for the acceptance by so many of the identity of the three women.

Lagrange deliberately limited himself to an examination of tradition concerning the women who anointed the Lord, and had in mind to make a further study of the Magdalene question, a study which, up to now, has not appeared. Urban Holzmeister examines most thoroughly the witnesses of ecclesiastical tradition.[2] He goes further than Lagrange by including in his studies the tradition concerning Mary Magdalene. It is true that, in the Latin Church, beginning with Ambrose, Augustine, and Cassian, the growth of the tradition increasingly leans to the one-person identification; but the oft-repeated assertion, that the teaching of the identity of the women who anointed the Lord is a "constans omnium veterum auctorum opinio" (Maldonat), "une tradition presque unanime" (Didon), "un sentiment général dans l'Eglise latine" (Fouard), "vigens opinio" (Corluy), can no longer be seriously made after the intensive studies of Lagrange and Holzmeister. The increasing tendency for the identity of the persons in the West is counterbalanced by an increasing tendency for their difference in the Patristic witnesses of the East. They did not stop with two women who anointed Jesus, but some admitted three, and isolated instances are found which admit even four women. Only in this way

[2]*Zeitschrift für kathol. Theol.* 46 (1922), pp. 402–22; 556–584.

did they believe it possible to explain the seemingly variant data concerning the supper at Bethany.

It would be superfluous to repeat at this time all the material of patristic times. It suffices merely to choose several witnesses of Christian antiquity whose declarations have a special significance in Biblical questions. For the rest, we may now refer to the works of the above-mentioned investigators.

Going back before the time of Gregory, we do not only find contradictory opinions among the various Fathers, but at times the same author in his writings upholds the oneness of persons, and again at other times stands for their distinction. In appraising the testimonies an error of method is committed by the supporters of the identity of persons as well as by those who support a distinction of persons. Frequently the text is too little examined as to whether the respective passage deals with the distinction of persons of the women who anointed the Lord, and thus it happens that the same patristic passages are used by both parties in support of their hypothesis. It occurs, too, that some individual Fathers are not stable in their views.

For Origen it is certain that the sinful woman (Luke 7) is different from Mary of Bethany;[3] the opposite view even seems entirely incredible to him: "Nec enim credibile est, ut Maria, quam diligebat Jesus, soror Marthae, quae meliorem partem elegerat, peccatrix in civitate fuisse vocatur."[4] Personally he is convinced that three women

---

[3] *Homil. 1, 4,* and *2, 2 in Cant.;* Migne, *P. gr.,* 13, 41, and 48; Baehrens, VIII, 33 and 43.

[4] *Comment. in Matth.,* Migne, *P. gr.,* 13, 1722. This is all the more striking since this same Origen, in his commentary on John, offers a different opinion. See Holzmeister, *loc. cit.,* p. 415.

anointed the Lord, and admits it possible that there may
have been four; "Certum est, quoniam aut sibi contraria
dicunt evangelistae, ut quidam eorum mentiantur; aut si
hoc impium est credere, necesse est dicere non de eadem
muliere omnes scripsisse evangelistas, sed aut de tribus
aut de quatuor."[5] The difficulty against the identification
of the women appears so great to him that he would
rather hold: "Principaliter evangelistarum propositum
fuit respiciens ad mysteria, et non satis curaverunt, ut
secundum veritatem enarrarent historiae, sed ut rerum
mysteria, quae ex historia nascebantur exponerent."[6]
Thereby Origen shows his preference for the Alexan-
drian trichotomy of Holy Scripture.

Ambrose is not clear on the case of the anointing
women, and purposely leaves the question undecided.[7]

Hilary definitely separates both women who anointed
the Lord.[8]

Augustine distinguishes two anointings, one in the
house of Simon the Pharisee, the other in the house of
Simon the Leper in Bethany. The accounts of the three
Evangelists Matthew, Mark, and John on the last
anointing afford us no grounds for accepting several
anointings at Bethany according to Augustine. He
would prefer to have both women looked upon as one.[9]

---

[5]*Ibid.*, 1723.

[6]*Ibid.*

[7]*Comment. in Luc.* 7; Migne, *P. lat.*, 15, 1671 ff.

[8]See Migne, *P. lat.*, 9, 748.

[9]*De cons. Evv.*, II, 154–56; Migne, *P. lat.*, 34, 1152–56. At least he
believed he would thus have to decide our question around the year
400. The considerations against identification, however, gave his
critical nature no rest, and thus fifteen years later the same opinion
seems doubtful to him. One passage in Sermon 105 is very difficult
to understand if Augustine at that time still held that Martha's sister

Jerome, the greatest exegete among the Fathers, makes a sharp distinction between the sinful woman and the one who anointed the Lord at Bethany: "Nemo putet eamdem esse, quae super caput effudit unguentum, et quae super pedes."[10] His opinion is most valuable because he was well acquainted with the local traditions

---

was the one-time sinful woman. He sees in the sisters an example of an earthly life full of troubles, and of a blessed life hereafter, and says: "Ambae innocentes, ambae laudabiles, una laboriosa, altera otiosa; nulla facinorosa, nulla disidiosa." Then he repeats the phrase: "Ambae innocentes, ambae inquam laudabiles." Preceding this there is a restrictive clause: "Vita vero iniqua aberat ab illa domo, nec cum Martha nec cum Maria; et si aliquando fuit, Domino intrante fugit." This restriction, however, need not be interpreted only in one sense as pointing to Mary's previous life of sin; for this would not have been spent in the house of Bethany and would not have first stopped at the visit of Jesus (Luke 10:38). His remark must be taken in a more general sense and is to be understood as referring to the faults found in every home where sinful people are wont to live. (Migne, *P. lat.*, 38, 618.) The opinion of the Bishop of Hippo, however, given in this text is not at all clear on our question, because in tract 49 on the Gospel of St. John he emphatically states his doubt concerning the identity of Mary of Bethany and the sinful woman. In spite of this, immediately following he calls her "famosa peccatrix," of whom it was said: "Many sins are forgiven her, because she has loved much" (Migne, *P. lat.*, 35, 1748). From the changing opinions of St. Augustine we can conclude that he cannot with justice be reckoned among those who stand unequivocally for the identification of the anointing women.

[10] *Comment. in Matth.*, Migne, *P. lat.*, 26, 191. The above words are so clear and exact that the following sentence: "Nec enim poterat statim capite Domini digna fieri meretrix," is not to be taken as meaning that the sinful woman later became worthy to anoint our Lord's head. Jerome would otherwise have upheld in the last sentence what he showed as incredible in the previous sentence. His commentary on Hoshea written some eight years later shows a confusion of the accounts of the anointing women. On account of its strong allegorical method of exposition, this testimony is of less value (Migne, *P. lat.*, 25, 817). For a more detailed presentation see Holzmeister, *loc. cit.*, 414.

of Palestine. John Chrysostom, too, the greatest homilist, while he also erroneously believes that the anonymous sinner of Luke is the same as the nameless woman who anointed our Lord at Bethany, mentioned by Matthew and Mark, decidedly rejects any identification of the sinful woman with Mary of Bethany.[11] This distinction is significant, for Chrysostom, being a master of the Greek language, knew that through the aorist of John 11:2 there was no reference to Luke 7:36 ff. In his commentary on John, he prefers three separate anointings performed by three different women, rather than to identify the pious sister of Martha with a sinful woman.[12]

Theodore of Mopsuestia, the friend of St. Chrysostom, is mentioned by Faillon as a witness for the identity of the anointing women. The testimony of such a critical mind from the school of Antioch would be of great value. But Faillon had the misfortune to draw his proofs from a work not ascribed to a definite Theodore. Theodore of Heraclea is meant, and not Theodore of Mopsuestia.[13]

The heading of the 93 homily of St. Peter Chrysologus offers a striking example of how arbitrarily at times the texts of the Fathers on our question have been distorted. In Migne's edition the title reads: "De conversione Magdalenae." In the homily itself, no mention of Magdalene is made. The narrative of Luke concerning the conversion of the sinful woman is explained without confusing the anonymous woman with the Magdalene. The codices show that this homily formerly bore the title: "De ea

---

[11]*Hom. 80* (81) *in Matt.,* Migne, *P. gr.,* 58, 723.
[12]*Hom. 62 in Jo.,* Migne, *P. gr.,* 59, 342.
[13]See Lagrange, *loc. cit.,* p. 325.

quae unxit Dominum unguento." The editor gave the
name to the anonymous woman, and thus made St.
Peter the author of the editor's own subjective opinion.[14]

What Ephrem the Syrian thought of our question is
hard to learn from the uncertain passages handed down
to us. This much is certain, though, that the Church
doctor did a great deal in confusing Biblical women. He
even confuses Mary Magdalene with Mary the Mother
of Jesus insofar as he permits the words "noli me tangere" in John 20:17 to be directed to the Mother of God.
Ephrem does, however, distinguish between the woman
who anointed the Lord's feet and her who anointed His
head. Further on, when he writes concerning Luke 10:36
ff., "Venit Maria et sedet ad pedes Jesu . . . ad pedes ejus
sedit, qui et mulieri peccatrici veniam dederat peccato-
rum," he clearly distinguishes Martha's sister from the
sinful woman.[15]

There is not a single testimony before the time of
Origen for the identification of both women who
anointed the Lord, based on John 11:2. This fact should
startle those who see in both aorist forms the strongest
evidence for the identification of Lazarus' sister with the
sinful woman. What was said above concerning Chrysostom might be said more or less of all the Greek
Fathers. Their intimacy with the language of the Gospels gave them no occasion to look upon the reference
of John 11:2 as pointing to the anointing of Jesus by the
sinful woman, and to assert that Mary of Bethany was
that woman. Tatian, an expert in harmonizing Gospel

---

[14]For further examples see U. Holzmeister, *op. cit.*, pp. 565–66; 576.
[15]See A. Merk, "Die Marien und salbenden Frauen bei Ephraem,"
in *Zeitschr. f. d. kath. Theol.*, 47 (1923), pp. 494–96.

narratives, did not hold Mary of Bethany and the sinner to be one and the same person. Irenaeus knows of no parallel passages in the other Evangelists corresponding to Luke 7:36 ff.[16] Thus the testimonies against the identity of the anointing women take us up into the second century, while the witnesses for their identification are of a later date. We may also correctly assert that many of the Fathers mention nothing of the anonymous sinner when they speak of Mary of Bethany, nor do they name the former when they mention the latter. And still, it would often have been easy to refer to her former sinful life or to point to the events in Bethany as an example of lasting conversion, had the Fathers not looked upon the women as distinct persons. This argument *e silentio* is strengthened by the return of present-day pulpit-literature to the older method.

Up to now the witnesses from tradition have been presented either for or against the identity of the two women who anointed the Lord. Little material can be found upholding the identity of persons, and there is even still less if we include Mary Magdalene and try to show that in Christian antiquity this follower of Jesus was identified either with the sinful woman, or with Mary of Bethany, or with both. Even those Fathers who acknowledge that Mary of Bethany and the sinful woman are one and the same person, never had the thought of confusing them with Mary Madgalene. Holzmeister has a long list of passages from the writings of the Greek, Syrian, and Latin Fathers which speak neither of the sinful woman nor of Martha's sister, but they do deal with Mary Magdalene, and would surely allude to

---

[16]*Adversus haer.*, III, 14, 3; Migne, *P. gr.*, 7, 916.

her identification with the foregoing if the authors had not considered the persons separate. This identification is especially valuable to the opponents of Christianity who occupy themselves with Mary Magdalene. Her testimony concerning the Lord's resurrection was very embarrassing to many. "How greatly could not the scoffers have made use of this fact that a one-time harlot was the first to gaze upon the Risen Lord!"[17] In order to overcome the difficulties of the account of the Resurrection, several Fathers admitted two Magdalenes; Hesychius of Jerusalem, even three. They would never have come upon this, if they had known Mary of Bethany and the sinful woman under the name of Mary Magdalene.

In our examination of the Gospel narratives, reference was made to the opinion of Faulhaber who distinguishes between the sinful woman and Martha's sister, but identifies her with Mary Magdalene. The distinguishing mark of the anonymous woman (Luke 7:36 ff.) known in the city as a sinner can only have the sense that this woman had given up her virginity for a price. But Ambrose and Modestus of Jerusalem give the title of "virgin" to Mary Magdalene and thus definitely distinguish her from the sinful woman. In a sermon falsely attributed to St. Augustine, Martha's sister is called "virgo prudentissima."[18] She also "has chosen the better part." By this honorable title the thought of the sinful woman is excluded. The abovementioned passage of St. Augustine wherein he praises Mary and Martha as types of two ways of living war-

[17]Holzmeister, loc. cit., p. 561.
[18]Migne, P. lat., 40, 1296.

rants a similar meaning: "ambae innocentes, ambae laudabiles . . . nulla facinorosa." Cyril of Alexandria in his explanation of John 20:17 distinguishes the Magdalene from the sinful woman; for she was permitted to touch Jesus, while the same was denied to Mary Magdalene.[19] We may also point to the Apostolic Constitutions 3, 6, where Mary Magdalene, Martha, and Mary are placed side by side.[20] Even though the present form of the Constitutions dates from the end of the fourth century or the beginning of the fifth, still much of the matter contained therein goes back much earlier.

Among the four different Marys mentioned in the Gospels, Theophylact makes mention of Mary of Bethany as well as Mary Magdalene.[21] Pseudo-Chrysostom knows five different Marys. In the Coptic text of the apocryphal "Discourses of Jesus with His disciples after the Resurrection," three sisters; Mary, Martha, and Mary Magdalene go to the tomb to anoint the body.[22]

Mary Magdalene plays an especially important role in the book *Pistis-Sophia* which seems to come from the third century. The Coptic text of this work is a valuable source for the study of Gnosticism. Therein Jesus Him-

---

[19]Migne, *P. gr.*, 74, 693.

[20]Migne, *P. gr.*, 1, 771 ff.

[21]Migne, *P. gr.*, 124, 862.

[22]Edgar Hennecke, *Neutest. Apokryphen* (Leipzig, 1904), 39. In the Ethiopian text the three women are called Sarrha, Martha, and Mary. Jesus first sends Martha, then Mary to the Apostles to announce His resurrection. Mary of Bethany in this work grouped with her sister Martha is clearly distinguished from Mary Magdalene. Carl Schmidt places the date of the composition of this work between A.D. 160–170. If this date is correct, then we would have a very early testimony for the non-identification. See Carl Schmidt, *Gespräche Jesu mit seinen Jüngern nach der Auferstehung* (Leipzig, 1919), 38 ff.; pp. 239, 402.

self repeatedly praises His disciple Mary Magdalene.[23] She surpasses by far all the other disciples and followers of the Lord, even the Mother of Jesus. She seems to be prepossessed with her own importance, for she speaks very often: in not less than 67 passages of the book she is the main personage to speak.[24] Peter must often entreat the Lord to silence the talkative woman, so that the disciples present may also say a few words: "My Lord, never shall we be able to tolerate this woman, for she takes our opportunities away from us, and she never permits any of us to speak, but she does so innumerable times."[25] It remains very doubtful whether Mary Magdalene is confused with Mary of Bethany in this book and identified with her. Her character portrayal does not harmonize with that of the modest sister of Martha. At most we may recognize in both persons the same eager effort to force themselves into the mysteries of God's Kingdom. On the other hand, an identity with the great sinner is not evident. The Magdalene is placed in order next to the Apostle John, and he is clearly called a virgin. John the virgin and Mary Magdalene will sit on the right and left of Jesus in heaven. For the rest, the *Pistis-Sophia* lays little stress on the historical characteristics of the personages. They are more or less instruments through which the Gnostic author presents his bizarre ideas.

---

[23]See Ad. Harnack, "Über das gnost. Buch Pistis-Sophia," in *Texte und Untersuchung*, VII, 2 (Leipzig, 1891), p. 15.

[24]See Carl Schmidt, "Gnostische Schriften in Koptischer Sprache," in *Texte und Untersuchung*, VIII, 1–2 (Leipzig, 1892), p. 452.

[25]*Ibid.*, p. 455. Schmidt employs an old Greek copy of *Pistis-Sophia*, and places it in the second half of the third century. *Zeitschr. f. d. Neutest. Wiss.*, 24 (1925), p. 232.

Formerly I expressed the opinion that Ephrem the Syrian (+373) was the first who ascribed the name Magdalene to the anonymous sinner.[26] Holzmeister[27] does not hold this to be certain, and only admits that the declaration of Ephrem "is only the first step in the beginning of the identification of the Magdalene with the sinful woman, which was later accepted in the Syrian Church." Nothing more can be proved from the words of Ephrem.

Holzmeister comes to the conclusion "that neither in the Eastern nor in the Western Church was there a tradition which considered Mary Magdalene the same person as the sister of Lazarus or as the sinful woman."[28]

We can finally find a traditional witness for the distinction of persons in the texts handed down and in older translations. It is a striking fact that no translation and no manuscript of the original text is guilty of mixing the various names. Had the copyists or translators been of the opinion that there was only one woman bearing the different names, there would surely be found a change in the use of these various names by one or the other, as is often the case in similar instances to the extent that even different outstanding persons of like name are confused. An example of such a textual change is that of the narrative of the banquet given by Simon the Pharisee (Luke 7:40 ff.) who is confused with Simon Peter; "et respondit Jesus ad Petrum . . . dixit illi Simon . . ." or "Petre, habeo tibi. . . . At ille respondit dicens: magister dic . . . Respondit Petrus . . . Propter

---

[26]"Noli me tangere," in *Pastor bonus*, 31 (1918–19), p. 273.
[27]Page 573.
[28]Page 579.

quod dico tibi, Petre."[29] If Mary of Bethany and Mary
Magdalene had been taken for the same person, how
easy it would have been to add the word Magdalene
where only the name Mary occurred; as in John 11:19,
20, 31, 32; 12:3; Luke 10:39.

If, in early Christendom, the same woman had been
known under three names, it would be difficult to see
how later there could arise a plurality of persons. But it
is easy to understand how in spite of the original distinction of the three persons they could in later genera-
tions be looked upon as one. The reason for this is found
in the misunderstanding of John 11:2, in the tendency
to harmonize texts, and not least in the predilection of
preachers and ascetical writers to seek concrete examples
in the Gospels.

After John 11:2 had served as a bridge for identifying
the sinful woman with Mary of Bethany, it was but a
step further for the homilists to unite this so-called Mary,
the one-time sinner, with the other Mary in the following of Jesus, particularly since the sevenfold possession
of this Mary of Magdala could be powerfully depicted
as a sign of great moral failings. Thus the person of the
Magdalene was turned into a living illustration of the
words of St. Paul (Rom. 5:20): "Where sin abounded,
grace did more abound." Jerome thus writes to Mar-
cella: "Maria Magdalena ipsa est, a qua septem daemo-
nia expulerat, ut ubi abundaverat peccatum, superabun-
daret gratia."[30] Carl Schmidt shows another way of making a combination which leads to their identification.
Not only in the *Pistis-Sophia* but also in other Gnostic

---

[29]See Theod. Zahn, *Das Evangelium des Lukas*, p. 323, note 24.
[30]*Epist. 59,* 4; Migne, *P. lat.,* 22, 588.

writings Mary Magdalene enjoys a particular respect. She is frequently not mentioned by her full name, but simply as Mary. Since she appears as Myrophore next to Mary and Martha, a confusion with Mary of Bethany was very easy.[31]

2. ECCLESIASTICAL OFFICE AND REPRESENTATION IN ART

There still remains a short reference to the office of the Church and the representations of art insofar as they enter into the question as witnesses of tradition. The axiom *Lex precandi lex credendi,* cannot be used in this case. Even if our present-day Breviary in the office of Mary Magdalene on July 22 clearly points to the sinful woman and Martha's sister, still theologians are not wanting who would like to declare this day as the general feast of the three distinct women, like the threefold commemoration on Epiphany of the Adoration of the Magi, the Baptism of Jesus in the Jordan, and the Miracle at Cana. Still the fact remains that the identity of the three women is supposed in the office of July 22. Is our question, therefore, decided? By no means. The office is of a comparatively late date. The antiphon of I Vespers shows how little claim is made of historical accuracy in the use of Scripture texts: The accounts of both anointings are confused. The scene is transferred from Galilee to Bethany, and Simon the Pharisee is confused with Simon the Leper. The Church herself has never vindicated the historical truth and accuracy of everything in the Lessons of the Second Nocturn, and in some antiphons and hymns. The same is

---

[31]Carl Schmidt, *Gespräche Jesu,* pp. 239–40.

true of the homilies in the Third Nocturn, as long as they do not deal with expositions of a unanimous tradition. Pope Pius X in his great Breviary reform planned a thorough revision of non-Biblical readings, a reform which because of the comprehensive preparatory work necessary could not quickly be carried out. Just the office of St. Mary Magdalene in his time was changed in several Ecclesiastical provinces of France and in the Cluniac Cloisters because in it "the three Marys" are confused into one. Through this the personal distinction was more strongly brought to the fore.

The critical researches of an Estius, Mabillon, and Ruinart had as their result the appearance in 1680 under Archbishop Harlay of Paris of a revised Breviary wherein the three women were sharply distinguished. Immediately the revision found much opposition; but the able defense of Claude Chastelain, the president of the commission, not only won new defenders for the opinion of the "three Marys," but went so far as to establish in a new office a special feast for Mary of Bethany on January 19. Even though this feast was soon suppressed through the efforts of P. Sellier and was combined with that of Martha and her brother Lazarus, acceptance of the view of three different women spread farther and farther. The researches of Calmet and the Breviary of Noailles did much to further the cause also.[32] As Estius remarks, Pope Clement VIII permitted a hymn to be taken out of the office of Mary Magdalene in which the identity of this saint with the other women was clearly expressed.[33]

---

[32]Didon, *Jésus Christ* (Paris, 1891), pp. 861–63.
[33]See Calmet, *Dissertationes*, III, pp. 189–90.

The Greeks even today celebrate the feast of the converted sinner on March 21 (in some places on March 19); on March 18 they celebrate the feast of Mary, the sister of Lazarus, and with the Latin Church the feast of Mary Magdalene on July 22. They also separate the celebrations of the anointing of Jesus by Mary of Bethany and that by the sinful woman. The Armenians celebrate a special feast of the brother and sisters of Bethany on the Monday following the sixth Sunday after the feast of the Exaltation of the Holy Cross, while they commemorate Mary Magdalene with the other Myrophores, after the octave of the Assumption of the Blessed Virgin Mary. The Copts have a commemoration of the two sisters Mary and Martha on 18 Tôbi (January), and a special feast of Mary Magdalene on 28 Epip (July). In the Mozarabic order of feasts only the calendar of Corduba, dating from the tenth century, has the feast of Mary Magdalene.[34]

Several old Martyrologies place the death and burial of Mary of Bethany and her sister Martha in Jerusalem, while Mary Magdalene's tomb is found in Ephesus.[35] Likewise Gregory of Tours, Modestus of Jerusalem, and Willibald of Eichstatt tell us of the Magdalene's tomb at Ephesus.[36] In a Veronese Missal the same Mary Mag-

---

[34]See Cabrol-Leclercq, *Monumenta Ecclesiae liturgica*, V (Paris, 1904), p. 473; also Nich. Nilles, *Kalendarium Manuale utriusque Ecclesiae*, II (Oeniponte: 1881), pp. 594; 611–12; 217; *Acta Sanctorum*, Probylaeum Novembris, pp. 833 f.; 551.

[35]See *Acta Sanctorum*, Julii V, 191; also Rietsch, *Die nachevangelische Geschichte der Bethan. Geschwister und die Lazarus-Reliquien zu Andlau*, Strassburg, 1902, pp. 53–56; Baumstark, in *Oriens christianus*, 2 (1902), pp. 471 ff.

[36]See H. Kellner, *Heortologie*[3] (Freiburg, 1911), p. 234.

dalene appears for the first time in the tenth century; in the Roman only in the thirteenth century. Up to the present Lazarus has as yet received no place in the Missal. In the Roman Martyrology he is mentioned on December 17. It is also noteworthy that the lessons in the office of Mary Magdalene contain nothing biographical, but simply the homilies of Gregory the Great, while in the lessons for St. Martha there are some accounts which were still unknown to Pseudo-Rhabanus.

In the Liturgy we can also observe that the oldest testimonies speak more for the difference than for the identity of the three women. In the flourishing period of *officia propria,* the differences of opinions on this question are especially clear in the liturgy. One cannot speak of a unanimous liturgical tradition in the Middle Ages. At the same time that the author of the *Dies Irae* wrote, "Qui Mariam absolvisti Et latronem exaudisti Mihi quoque spem dedisti," and gave the name Mary to the converted sinner (the Magdalene or Mary of Bethany?), a Mozarabic *Exorcismus* places Mary Magdalene with the virgins.[37] In the Litany of All Saints, which dates back at least to the fifth century in its oldest form, Mary Magdalene is invoked as a virgin, and her name stands at the beginning of the holy virgins. There is no thought of her being a widow. Therefore there is real significant liturgical testimony for the distinction between the sinful woman and the Magdalene, which coincides with the designation of Mary Magdalene as a virgin by Ambrose and Modestus of Jerusalem.[38]

Oftentimes the representations of art have a great value

---

[37] See Cabrol-Leclercq, *Monumenta,* V, p. 523.
[38] *Ibid.*

as witnesses of tradition. Not seldom the mural paint-
ings of the catacombs and of the oldest church buildings
offer strong support for dogmatical, liturgical, and historical questions. But, unfortunately ancient art leaves
our question for the most part undecided. Mary Magdalene is, indeed, represented in early art with the pious
women at the Lord's tomb. The scene of the anointing
of Jesus also drew the attention of the early Christian
artist, since it furnished him with splendid motives. One
cannot conclude, however, that in the ancient representations of Biblical scenes concerned, the narratives of the
Evangelists on the various women are combined to
point to one woman. Later on, it is true, things change.[39]
Heinrich Detzel is a little too apodictic in his judgment
when he states: "Christian art from the earliest times
held fast to one person."[40] In a picture in the lower
church of SS. Cosmas and Damian at Rome, the event
in the house of Simon the Pharisee narrated in Luke
7:36 ff. is vividly portrayed. It is easy to recognize the
sinful woman. Wilpert believes that in a second picture
of the same lower church, the same woman is again
shown at the grave of Jesus. According to Wilpert the
artist openly took the sinner for Mary Magdalene. Since
both pictures, however, date only from the thirteenth
century, they have little value as witnesses of tradition.
The identification of Mary, the sister of Martha with
the sinner is very distinct in a miniature of a Parisian
codex of homilies, for there Mary is called ἡ πορνή. Both

---

[39]See Jos. Wilpert, *Die römischen Mosaiken u. Malereien,* II (Text),
pp. 802–06; "Über die Frauen am Grabe," *ibid.,* pp. 901–05, with
the accompanying plates.

[40]Heinr. Detzel, *Christl. Ikonographie,* II (Freiburg, 1896), p. 514.

anointing scenes are also blended into one in the representation.[41] A mosaic at Monreale likewise identifies
Mary Magdalene with the converted sinner. Interesting
is a miniature in the Egbert-Kodex. On it appears not
only Mary, but also Martha with loose-flowing hair.
Did the artist thereby refer to the old manner of life of
the "delicati" as Wilpert supposes, or do they refer rather
to the above-mentioned sabbatical regulations?

The pictures referred to are older than the portrayal
of the banquet at the home of Simon the Pharisee by
Giovanni da Milano in S. Croce at Florence, which
Detzel claims to be the oldest, although it is of the
fourteenth century. The picture nevertheless is interesting for us because it connects Luke 7:36 ff. with 8:2.
While the sinful woman anoints the feet of Jesus, seven
devils are seen leaving the house through the roof.

That Mary Magdalene appears only under the cross
is in agreement with the development of the crucifixion
scenes. In the West we first come across these in the fifth
century.[42] As companion figures, the two thieves are
first depicted. (This is seen on the famous wooden door
of St. Sabina on the Aventine, in the oldest surviving
crucifixion group in the West); then the Mother of
Jesus, and John; farther off Longinus; sometimes soldiers
casting lots for the garments of the Crucified; and at
times our first parents Adam and Eve or only Adam
standing at the foot of the cross. Not beginning at the
time of Giotto, as Detzel asserts,[43] but even before we

[41]See Wilpert, *op. cit.*, p. 804.

[42]See Künstle, *Ikonographie der Heiligen,* I (Freiburg, 1928),
p. 446.

[43]See Detzel, II, p. 517.

find Mary Magdalene among the persons beneath the cross. But this can scarcely be claimed as proof that the earliest artists in these pictures wished to characterize Mary Magdalene as the converted sinner. Even if she is shown in these pictures, or alone with a cruse of ointment in her hand or at her feet, it does not follow that the artist took her for the sinner or Mary of Bethany. The cruse of ointment might just as well refer to the part played by the Magdalene in the embalming of the corpse in which, as the Evangelists narrate, she wished to share. Mary belongs to the Myrophores without being the sinful woman.

The case is different when we consider the pictures of the later Middle Ages, of the Renaissance, and of modern times. In them Mary Magdalene is shown under the cross and in other Biblical scenes so definitely as the converted sinner that there is no doubt that the artist took both persons to be one. It must be admitted that from an artistic viewpoint there is a very practical motive for this identification, that, namely of presenting the power of the expiatory death of Jesus for fallen mankind, especially since through the artistic restriction of place the penitent thief cannot be so adequately portrayed. The crouching figure of a woman at the foot of the cross offers a better theme as a symbol of the redeemed than the perpendicular crosses standing side by side without a tempering of the vertical lines. Often one greatly wishes that the representation of the Magdalene really as the converted sinner were a more fitting constituent of the impressive sacred Crucifixion scene. This wish manifests itself still more in regard to a more religious and less naturalistic perception in many pictures which, in agreement with the Provençal tradition, represent Magdalene as a penitent hermit. Against such "religious" portrayals are directed the sharp words of Wessely: "The artists are desirous of showing a beautiful nude feminine bust; an ointment-cruse, a skull, a cross in a corner accompany the figure of Mary Magdalene. Her seductive eyes and attitude remind us rather of an unconverted than a penitent disciple."[44]

A characteristic exemplar of many pictures of the Magdalene, since the Renaissance, is "a beautiful penitent Magdalene," which in the Autumn of 1531 Duke Frederick Gonzaga of Mantua caused to be executed by Titian, which painting is preserved in the Pitti Palace at Florence. The representation is distinguished for its voluptuous, sensual colors and drawing, but is devoid of all religious character. Such pictures have nothing in common with the Magdalene as we know her from the Gospels.

Since the beginning of the Middle Ages, Mary Magdalene has received great veneration as the patroness of penitents. In private votive chapels, her pictures adorned the altar. That was an age of great faith, and although not entirely free from moral failings, still it recognized sin as sin, and did severe penances in atonement. Such a generation took the Magdalene pictures seriously. But concerning the pictures of later times Karl Künstle correctly remarks, and in this agrees with Wessely: "The Baroque style of art grossly misused the motive, and one would take the seminude form of the prostrate woman for a prostitute if the crucifix and skull did not convey

---

[44] Acc. to C. Burg, in *Realenzyklop. f. prot. Theol. u. Kirche*, XII², p. 337.

the idea that the scene is a religious one. Pinturicchio already paved the way for such a representation when he depicted her in a painting in Aracoeli in Rome as being in the desert where she is visited by many distinguished young men. Luke van Leyden, in an engraving, shows her as a dancer in a lascivious company. Mark Koffermanns reproduces this scene in a large painting."[45]

All pictures on which the Magdalene is shown as the penitent presuppose a widespread acceptation of the opinion of her identity with the sinful woman of Luke's Gospel. They play an important role in the growing popularization of the identity of the women and in the almost entire suppression in the popular mind of their distinction. What the people saw daily before their eyes made a deep impression upon them, and it did not occur to them that nothing is to be found in the Gospels for this variously motivated identification. Not satisfied with the Biblical narrations, artists at times took passages from the legends of the penitent St. Mary of Egypt and with them enriched the picture of the Biblical Mary of Magdala.

In the same way as painting and plastic art wrought their effect, so poetry has done, and still does, much in a very wide field to bring it about that the name Mary Magdalene is taken without question to denote a converted public sinner. Many would be embarrassed were they called upon to justify this association of ideas, and would probably answer that this is the general conception. If prose and poetry were content to unite the individual characteristics of the three Biblical women in

---

[45]Karl Künstle, *Ikonographie der Heiligen*, II (Freiburg, 1926), p. 428.

their character portrayal of the Magdalene, and at least produce a womanly character, which, after her conversion, is fitted for the circle of disciples of the God-man, then nothing more could be said against this poetic freedom than can be said against the identification of the three women in general. This indeed is the case in most Passion plays and other religious dramas. But the same cannot be said of many modern works. As models must sit for the artist if a "beautiful sinner" is to be painted, whose grace is to be piquant, since he is dealing with a Biblical woman, so many poets turn to the Magdalene theme in order to find material for morbid scenes and erotic entanglements even in the company of Jesus. This is true not only of authors of a recognized degenerate literature, but also of writers who have a good reputation in the field of literature. J. Leipoldt remarks: "Mary of Magdala is a favorite topic among poets (not the historical Mary, but the one in the legends): I recall Paul Heyse's *Mary of Magdala,* John Schlaf's *Jesus and Mirjam,* Maurice Maeterlinck's *Mary Magdalene,* Rainer Maria Rilkes' *Love of the Magdalene.* All these works are not only poems on Mary; they wish still more to give honor to Him who said: 'Let him that is without sin cast the first stone.' "[46] Paul Heyse contents himself with showing the Magdalene as the beloved of the traitor Judas. F. Hebbel presents Mary Magdalene as the "beloved of the youthful Christ. She loves Him, and since she cannot bear to be rejected by Him, for as she reasons: I must be unworthy of Him, she falls into sin, makes herself unworthy of Him, but is thereby drawn to God and to God in Him." The theme of Richard

---

[46]From *Jesusbilde der Gegenwart*[2] (Leipzig, 1925), pp. 30-31.

Wagner's *Jesus of Nazareth* is similar.[47] Hebbel's
Christ, in which these thoughts were to be worked
out, remained in outline form. John Schlaf goes a step
further and has the harlot Mirjam (Mary Magdalene)
become the dangerous temptress of Jesus. For every be-
liever in Christ the amorous poem of Richard Dehmel
Jesus Begs is intolerable. In this poem the author has
the Redeemer beg for proofs of Mary's love in verses
full of disgusting sensuality.[48] What the deadly enemies
of Christ dared not befoul during His lifetime, these
German poets drag into the mire of their impure imagination. It is but one step to the blasphemous, bungling
work of the prize-winner, W. Hasenclever *Marriages
are consummated in Heaven* wherein Mary plays the
role of the converted sinner, or better unconverted, for
in heaven she continues her seductive machinations.
These infamous products of an age submerged in sen-
sualism are mentioned here, only because it is through
them that some become acquainted with the Magdalene
question, and are influenced in their opinion on the identification of Mary Magdalene with the sinful woman.
They seldom gather their knowledge from the Bible;
and still more seldom from sermons and positive religious writings.

With more poetic license Renée Erdos in her drama
John the Disciple makes Mary Magdalene the second
main personage as the former betrothed of the Beloved
Disciple.[49] When John renounces the world, Mary Magdalene falls "a prey to vice." She is converted and does

---

[47]See Leipoldt, p. 31.

[48]See the text in Leipoldt, *loc. cit.,* p. 53.

[49]Translated into German by John Mumbauer (Mainz, 1920).

penance for her sins. But the love for John inflames her anew, until all earthly passion becomes purified in the sacrifice which John together with her brings with complete resignation to the Crucified Master. This poem of the Hungarian Jewess convert to the Catholic Faith, despite many gems of thought, is unbiblical and arouses misgivings. Its poetical value will so much the more promote and make secure the association of ideas that makes Mary Magdalene to be the great sinner.

When, therefore, a representation has entered the mind from so many sources, it is not easy to set up against it another representation, which has weaker appeal to many, because it establishes by soberer proof the main truth; and because it is not the creation of the resources of poetic art; and because it is able to offer less piquant motifs to the artist.

III. THE MAGDALENE QUESTION IN PRESENT-DAY BIBLICAL CRITICISM

Formerly it was considered a sign of a somewhat suspected and weak sacred exegesis for anyone to accept and defend the opinion of the distinct women in the Magdalene question, as the previously mentioned censure of Lefèvre's work by the Sorbonne shows. The situation has changed at present. The majority of Catholic exegetes stand for the separate individuality of the women, if not for three, at least for two.[50] Even fundamentalist Protestant investigators hold fast to the distinction of three persons and two anointings. It is most singular that even at first glance we gain the impression that the ever-increasing number of believers in Revelation who defend the unity of person of the three women coincides with the extreme rationalistic interpreters of the Gospels. A closer examination shows this to be a natural consequence, since both parties set out from an entirely different point and are actuated by opposite motives. Up to

---

[50] Besides the authors mentioned as defenders of two or three persons in the Magdalene-question by Holzmeister, *Zeitschr. f. kath. Theol.*, 46 (1922), pp. 404–406, we may add: E. Dimmler, *Das Evan. nach Lukas;* M. Gladbach (1911), pp. 105–106; Cl. Fillion, *Vie de N. S. Jésus-Christ*, II (Paris, 1922), pp. 333; 592–593; Pölxl-Innitzer, *Leidens- und Verklärungsgeschichte³* (Graz, 1925), pp. 13–14; Jos. Sickenberger, *Bibl. Zeitschrift*, 17 (1925–26), pp. 63–74; W. Müller, *Der Fels*, 21 (1926–27), pp. 85–94; 131–138; L. Fonck, *Verbum Domini*, 8 (1928), pp. 65–74.

now we have analyzed the opinions of the first group. A short reference to the later and latest hypotheses of rationalistic criticism is demanded.

In the history of religion, some have attempted to show that the various Biblical accounts deal with the same person, who really did not exist, but who only forms a legendary counterpart similar to the mythical figures in the life of great religious founders. Rud. Seydel follows this procedure in his endeavor to find all possible parallels between Buddha and Christ and thereby to prove the dependence of the Gospels on Buddhistic legends; even Luke 7:36 ff. is compared to the visit to Buddha by the courtesan Ambupâli.[51] In order to accomplish this, the investigator of Buddhism had to identify Mary of Bethany with the sinner in Luke's Gospel and not only that, but he confused Luke 7:36 ff. with 10:38 ff. C. Clemen also accuses Seydel of this error, but he himself believes that "the Gospel of St. John identifies the Mary of Luke with the woman who anointed Jesus at Bethany."[52] The peak of the license of criticism up to this time is unquestionably reached by Jensen when he also confuses Luke 7:36 ff. with 10:38 ff. in which he sees a counterpart for the marriage of Eabanis with Hierodule, and calls the banquet in Bethany the wedding feast of Jesus with Mary of Bethany.[53] The rejection of this opinion by Clemen is still too mild: "One must not be provoked at this, that

---

[51]Rud. Seydel, *Das Evangelium Jesu in seinen Verhältnissen zur Buddhasage und Buddhalehre*[2] (Weimar, 1897), p. 185 f.

[52]C. Clemen, *Religions-geschichtliche Erklärung des Neuen Test.* (Giessen, 1909), p. 256.

[53]P. Jensen, *Das Gilgamesch Epos in der Weltliteratur*, I (Strassburg, 1906), p. 981.

Jensen sees only legends in the Gospel story of Jesus, and yet one does not know how to refute such argumentation."[54] The reader will notice that Jensen himself, in the preface to his book, on page ix, writes that he is happy if, by good fortune, his "vivid imagination at times should have broken the bounds of strict logic." Under such circumstances the reader can hardly be astonished at anything that follows.[55]

Meanwhile Jensen was surpassed in religious historical arbitrary creations by Julius Grill. According to him, in the pericopes touching Mary Magdalene, Mary of Bethany, and the sinful woman, we have by all the indications to deal with a whole circle of variations of the theme of the Dawn and the Evening.[56] By the name Mary we have before us the sunrise — "the dawn of a new day." In natural agreement with it is the totally isolated reference of Luke 8:2 according to which, out of Mary called Magdalene seven devils have been driven (Mark 16:9). We readily infer that in the system of the religion of nature these spirits represent the darkness of the night; that they are seven in antithesis to the seven highest gods of the heavenly light;[57] and that their expulsion must be the work of the sun, of whose sevenfold rays the Veda repeatedly speaks; and whose New Testa-

---

[54]*Loc. cit.*, p. 221.

[55]Dausch, *Die drei älteren Evangelien* (Bonn, 1918), p. 444, sees in this a characteristic trait of modern Polemics which no longer shrinks from degrading the person of Jesus by interpreting the relation of Jesus with the women of Galilee and His friends from Bethany in the most shameful manner. In this rationalistic Bible criticism and sensualistic poetry agree.

[56]Julius Grill, *Untersuchungen über die Entstehung des vierten Evang.*, II (Tübingen, 1932), p. 178.

[57]Cf. the *adityas* of the Veda.

ment counterpart is believed to be Christ.[58] According to Grill, the interpretation of the name Magdalene as "hair dresser" probably identifies her with Mary of Bethany and the nameless sinner. Because of the apparition of Jesus to Magdalene on Easter morn, and also because of the representation in Arabic and Ethiopian texts as a combatant "she was originally the genius of the fighting daylight, which is held captive during the night by devils, which is freed by the sun, and first of all looks upon the risen daystar."[59] We need not cite the meanings of the other names in our pericopes as set forth by Grill. The above is sufficient to demonstrate the unrestrained arbitrariness of such explanations. If Mary signifies the dawn freed by the sun, how can she at the same time be the twilight which "carries off the sun"?[60]

Also how can she as the morning dawn drive away the night, the enemy of light, when she is represented as the light of day possessed by the demons of the night? Contrariwise how can she as the dawn carry off the light of the stars, and be an enemy of the light, when she represents the daylight held captive by the demons of the night? In the new edition of his work Clemen justly declares: "All that [Grill's hypotheses] is extraordinarily improbable . . . all is extraordinarily farfetched."[61]

The adherents of the historico-critical method and of the theory of historical formulation wish to solve our

[58]*Ibid.*, pp. 179–180.

[59]*Ibid.*, p. 181.

[60]*Ibid.*, p. 183.

[61]Carl Clemen, *Religions-geschichtliche Erklärung des Neuen Test.* (Giessen, 1924), pp. 232, 234.

problem by textual criticism and evolution to prove that
in ancient tradition there was mention only of one
anointing of Jesus. "Most of these critics assert that the
event in Luke 7:36 ff. is a later form of the account
touching the anointing in Bethany."[62] According to John
Weiss the event concerning the sinful woman and Mary
of Bethany belong to the proper parts of Luke's Gospel; i.e., to those parts not found in Matthew and Mark,
which are designated by the siglum S.[63] Only the anointing related by Luke has been borrowed from Mark
14:3-9, also perhaps the name of the host Simon. "For
the rest both narrations are entirely different."[64] If we
take the anointing out of the account of Luke, because
according to Weiss it "not only can be entirely dispensed
with, but gives to the scene a strange characteristic,"
then nothing more perfect can be built up: "Luke's narration is original, and one of the most beautiful of the
proper parts."[65] Erich Klostermann ascribes it to Luke's
preference for penitent sinners, that he in 7:36 ff. de-
velops the distorted one original text of Mark 14:3 ff.
"In the former (Luke 7:36 ff.) the subject of a sinner
in the house of one clean — Simon the Pharisee; in the
latter (Mark 14:3 ff.) that of a disciple in the house of
one unclean — Simon the Leper; in the first case no
murmuring over the waste and no prediction of the
death of Jesus; in the second case no forgiveness and no
address to the woman, etc."[66]

[62]John Weiss, *Die Schriften des Neuen Test.*, I², p. 450.

[63]*Ibid.*, p. 408.

[64]*Ibid.*, p. 451.

[65]*Ibid.*, p. 450.

[66]Erich Klostermann, *Lukas* (Tübingen, 1919), p. 454; also, *Das
Markus-Evangelium*² (Tübingen, 1926), pp. 158–160.

W. Bousset and H. Gressman view in the narrative
of the sevenfold possession of the Magdalene (Luke 8:2;
Mark 16:9) an expression of the Jewish belief in demons,
as it appears in the apocryphal Testaments. The author
"admits seven (or eight) spirits, from which spring the
seven capital sins."[67] O. Holtzmann believes John 11:2
a reference to the anointing by the sinful woman nevertheless. The fourth Evangelist misplaces the same event
at Bethany. "Thus two different events seem to have
been confused at an early period."[68] "Here the error in
John's Gospel is obvious."[69] W. Bauer judges otherwise.
He says it is noteworthy that John 11:2 "refers to an
event which we shall meet later on (John 12:1–8). Still
we know the practice of the Evangelists to look back
from their standpoint without concerning themselves
with it any more."[70] John is made to borrow the
statement of the wiping with the hair from the account
of the anointing by the sinful woman, even if in Bethany
"it is a little out of place."[71] L. v. Sybel declares the
anointing by Mary of Bethany in John's Gospel to be a
confusion of Matthew and Mark, whereby Luke makes
embellishments and John adds his own new matter.
"Consequently to the fourth Evangelist the person in
the first two synoptics who anoints the Lord is identical
with the woman in the third and his own Gospel. For
him it deals with one and the same person and with one

[67]*Die Religion des Judentums im späthellenistischen Zeitalter*[3]
(Tübingen, 1926), p. 339.

[68]*Das Neue Testament*, I (Giessen, 1926), p. 260.

[69]*Ibid.*, II, p. 1017.

[70]*Das Johannes-Evangelium*[2] (Tübingen, 1925), p. 143.

[71]*Ibid.*, p. 153.

and the same incident — a second version of the scene."[72]
Luke undertakes the first narration of it and that very
imperfectly. The forgiving of sins served as a motive for
him to bring in the history of the anointing by the person of the great sinner. The anointing would, therefore,
be primary. "The narrative touching the sinful woman
may contain valuable thoughts, nevertheless its literary
style and form are inferior. It begins and ends in patch-
work. It is an inferior work, and based on the anointing in Bethany."[73] Sybel holds the exactly opposite position from that of Klostermann. Jülicher[74] and Bult-
mann,[75] have different solutions. Thus the results of later
Gospel criticism are unsatisfactory in the solution of the
Magdalene question. The problem cannot be solved by
history of religion, textual criticism, or by historical
formulation.

Many pastors perhaps shrink from a practical consideration of the distinction of the three women: Do we
not lose valuable material for preaching, catechizing,
and moral instruction, if we no longer consider Mary
Magdalene the converted sinner who remains faithful to
the Lord beneath the cross and even to the tomb? Yes
and no. Yes, insofar as the event in the house of Simon
the Pharisee may no longer be looked upon as the account of the Magdalene's conversion, and Luke 10:38 ff.
no longer used as a reference to the Saviour's kindness
in dealing with the former sinner, or also as an example
of how sincere the repentance of the sinful woman was,

---

[72]Die Salbungen, in *Zeitschrift f. d. neutest. Wiss.*, 23 (1924), p. 193.
[73]*Ibid.*, p. 186.
[74]*Die Gleichnisreden Jesu*, II, p. 290 ff.
[75]*Geschichte der synoptischen Tradition* (Göttingen, 1921), p. 10.

who now finds her greatest joy in listening to the word of God thereby forgetting all things earthly; while formerly her passions drove her from sin to sin so that she herself gave up all claim to honor and her good name. But the preacher personally convinced of the identity of the sinful woman and the Magdalene, in handling the above theme, must refrain from announcing this identity simply as the substance of divine Revelation, since many of his listeners may have read or heard that this is a controverted question. On the other hand, it would be equally wrong to present this and similar controverted questions to the people from a negative side, and thereby cause doubts in the minds of the faithful where heretofore none existed. This would add nothing to the instruction or training of the faithful. I accept with perfect accord the opinion of Leop. Fonck: "Tales enim quaestiones ex pulpito coram populo non sunt tractandae."[76]

Should these beautiful passages in the Gospels, therefore, be used less for edification and instruction than they were up to now? By no means. We should only represent the scenes as the Evangelists themselves describe them, and we should strive to get the most out of the great store of ideas contained in each account. In the conversion of the sinful woman (Luke 7:36 ff.), in the visit of Jesus with the sisters and brother at Bethany (Luke 10:38 ff.), in the conduct of Mary and Martha at the death of their brother (John 11), and at the farewell banquet at Bethany (John 12), in the accounts of the Magdalene's condition before her joining the company of Jesus (Luke 8:2; Mark 16:9), her faithful fol-

[76]Leopold Fonck, "Cena Bethanica," in *Verbum Domini*, 8 (1928), p. 74.

lowing and care for the bodily welfare of Jesus and His disciples (Luke 8:3; Mark 15:41; Matt. 27:55 f.), her perseverance under the cross and the touching love which she manifested at the tomb (Mark 15:40, 47; 16:1 ff.; Matt. 27:55 f., 61; 28:1 ff.; Luke 23:49, 55 f.; 24:1 ff.; John 19:25; 20:1 ff.) — in all these passages the preacher will find so many valuable lessons and thoughts of various kinds that he can very well refrain from building up any subjective theory out of the common relation of the above-mentioned texts.

In conclusion let us refer to the possibility that we may venerate Mary Magdalene as an example of true repentance even though she be not the same person as the sinful woman who anointed the Lord's feet.

It is mentioned twice that Mary Magdalene before her attachment to Jesus as one of His disciples was possessed by seven demons, and was freed from them by Jesus (Luke 8:2; Mark 16:9). It has already been said above that this declaration is to be understood as real possession and not as a figurative signification for a life of sin or even as a declaration of the seven capital sins. Nothing justifies us to conclude that those possessed always fall under the power of the devil as a consequence of previous sins. But the possibility of such a casual connection cannot be disputed. Let us examine the case of the Magdalene. We do not know what kind of sins we should have to ascribe to her. In this instance the sins of impurity must be at once dismissed, for the designation of Mary Magdalene as a "virgin" in the testimonies already cited disproves this. After the devils had once taken possession of her, she was no longer the mistress of her will and actions; nor was she subjectively guilty of objective sinful acts as a normal person is.[77] The anguish that must have filled the body and soul of the woman possessed by seven demons can be understood by observing the sufferings of a person possessed by only one devil. Mary Magdalene was freed from this suffering by Jesus, and showed her gratitude for this great benefit by becoming a follower of the Messiah. From the short accounts found in both Evangelists we cannot know for certain the moral condition of Mary before her cure. We should do an injustice to the zealous follower of Jesus if we should declare the possibility an actuality. But the above hypothesis finds no authorization either in Holy Scripture or in Tradition. If the opinion of Mary's sinful life and her just punishment by possession were proved without identifying her with the sinful woman in Luke and Mary of Bethany, then the consoling example of a converted sinner under the cross should be preserved for us in the person of Mary Magdalene.

The sinful woman who anointed our Lord once and for all remains hidden in the darkness of anonymity.

---

[77] Anne Katherine Emmerich in her considerations on the life of Jesus describes at length the condition of the Magdalene. After her first conversion, the public sinner relapses into her sinful life until Jesus releases her from the devil's power. The Magdalene then begs Him for protection lest she again fall into her former life. Jesus gives her the assurance of perseverance and says to the other disciples: "She was a great sinner, but she shall also forever be a model for all penitents." (Pustet, Regensburg, 1858, II, p. 249.) The mystic of Dülmen holds to the identity of the three women. Her vision can lay no claim to historical accuracy where it exceeds the Biblical accounts or even contradicts them. (See M. Meinertz, *"Anna Katharina Emmerich und das Neue Testament,"* in *Theol. Revue,* 28, 1929, pp. 97–104.)

Mary of Bethany, the virtuous sister of Martha and Lazarus, is free from the stain of a past that is not in accord with her chaste character as portrayed for us by the Evangelists. Mary Magdalene, freed from seven demons by Christ, belongs to the group of Galilean women in the company of the Lord who administered to Him from their substance. She lives on through the centuries as Magdala's most distinguished citizen. Every one of these three women has a right to be considered as a separate person and to be venerated as a saint.

www.ingramcontent.com/pod-product-compliance
Lightning Source LLC
LaVergne TN
LVHW091203080426
835509LV00006B/800